THIS BOOK BELONGS TO

_____

_____

START DATE _____ / _____ / _____

HE READS TRUTH

FOUNDERS

FOUNDER
Raechel Myers

CO-FOUNDER
Amanda Bible Williams

EXECUTIVE

CHIEF EXECUTIVE OFFICER
Ryan Myers

CHIEF OPERATING OFFICER
Mark D. Bullard

EDITORIAL

MANAGING EDITOR
Lindsey Jacobi, MDiv

PRODUCTION EDITOR
Hannah Little, MTS

ASSOCIATE EDITOR
Kayla De La Torre, MAT

COPY EDITOR
Becca Owens, MA

CREATIVE

SENIOR ART DIRECTOR
Annie Glover

DESIGN MANAGER
Kelsea Allen

DESIGNERS
Savannah Ault
Mackenzie Peters
Ashley Phillips

OPERATIONS

OPERATIONS DIRECTOR
Allison Sutton

OPERATIONS MANAGER
Mary Beth Steed

GROUP SALES AND ENGAGEMENT SPECIALIST
Karson Speth

OPERATIONS ASSISTANT
Emily Andrews

MARKETING

MARKETING DIRECTOR
Whitney Hoffmann

GROWTH MARKETING MANAGERS
Katie Bevels
Blake Showalter

PRODUCT MARKETING MANAGER
Krista Squibb

CONTENT MARKETING STRATEGIST
Tameshia Williams, ThM

SOCIAL MEDIA SPECIALIST
Bella Ponce

MARKETING SPECIALIST
Bailey Majewski

COMMUNITY ENGAGEMENT

COMMUNITY ENGAGEMENT MANAGER
Delaney Coleman

COMMUNITY ENGAGEMENT SPECIALISTS
Cait Baggerman
Katy McKnight

SHIPPING

SHIPPING MANAGER
Marian Welch

FULFILLMENT LEAD
Kajsa Matheny

FULFILLMENT SPECIALISTS
Hannah Lamb
Kelsey Simpson

CONTRIBUTORS

ARTWORK
Abbey Ratcliff

SUBSCRIPTION INQUIRIES
orders@hereadstruth.com

COLOPHON

This book was printed in Nashville, Tennessee, on 60# Lynx Opaque Text under the direction of He Reads Truth. Cover is 100# Cougar Opaque with a soft touch lamination.

COPYRIGHT

© 2025 by He Reads Truth, LLC
All rights reserved.

All photography used by permission.

ISBN 978-1-962221-21-4

1 2 3 4 5 6 7 8 9 10

No part of this publication may be reproduced, distributed, or transmitted in any form or by any means, including photocopying, recording, or other electronic or mechanical methods, without the prior written permission of He Reads Truth, LLC, except in the case of brief quotations embodied in critical reviews and certain other noncommercial uses permitted by copyright law.

All Scripture is taken from the Christian Standard Bible®. Copyright © 2020 by Holman Bible Publishers. Used by permission. Christian Standard Bible® and CSB® are federally registered trademarks of Holman Bible Publishers.

Though the dates, locations, and individuals in this book have been carefully researched, scholars disagree on many of these topics.

Research support provided by Logos Bible Software™. Learn more at logos.com.

HEREADSTRUTH.COM   @HEREADSTRUTH   Download the He Reads Truth app, available for iOS and Android

HE WILL SAVE US
A LENTEN STUDY OF ISAIAH

SOMEONE IS COMING
TO FORGIVE IT ALL.

WELCOME LETTER

Have you ever been indebted to someone? Maybe you've felt the weight of real monetary debt, or you've been treated with undeserved kindness by a friend you've wronged. Or perhaps you've had someone indebted to you, and you've had to wrestle with the decision between demanding repayment or wiping another's slate clean. Regardless of the circumstance, the feeling of being in debt is a heavy, often uncomfortable, weight to carry.

This is why one of the ways Scripture shows us how sin affects our relationship with God is through the concept of debt. The discomfort of owing something to a God who is holy, good, and perfect in every way—a God who is not in debt to us and a God that we can never pay back—is a difficult reality to live in. Yet this is one of the undercurrents of the season of Lent. It asks us to look at what sin truly costs and, in doing so, calls out a well of gratitude in us for what it took to restore us before God—a gratitude that we might not fully grasp if we do not understand the cost.

The season of Lent encourages us to look back before we look forward. It's about holding our eyes open, looking fully at our sin, and then keeping them open wide to fully comprehend the hope of Jesus that is coming. In this season we're invited to walk toward our hope, but we must remind ourselves of the beginning. We review our charges and repent of all we cannot begin to pay. And thus, we approach the cross with the gratitude of a sinner forgiven. No longer debtors, but by the grace of God, sons and daughters—coheirs of an eternal inheritance.

In the book of Isaiah, God's people are asked to do the same. The prophet took the time to show the people of Judah the destructiveness of their sin and its consequences. Line by line, he showed them the severity of their debt. But he also prophesied: someone is coming to forgive it all.

We're so grateful to take this journey with you for another year—to read the book of Isaiah and the Holy Week passages and acknowledge our mortality. We need Jesus. And as we approach the cross and the resurrection that will surely follow, we have this assurance: God will save His people.

THE HE READS TRUTH TEAM

DESIGN ON PURPOSE

Each He Reads Truth resource is thoughtfully and artfully designed to highlight the beauty, goodness, and truth of Scripture in a way that reflects the themes of each curated reading plan.

This Lenten Reading Guide features work from abstract expressionist artist Abbey Ratcliff. The scenes in Abbey's work contain darker tones and shades contrasted with strong highlights that together remind us of both the shadowy depths of sin and the hope of restoration for God's people. Using acrylics and different textural methods, her compositions are often built through a layering process that requires trust and patience. This process reflects the themes and warnings found in Isaiah; layer by layer God's people must trust in Him alone for their redemption.

The high contrast serif font we used preserves an air of timelessness while also nodding to the strength of the Lord and His call for holy living.

HOW TO USE THIS BOOK

He Reads Truth is a community of men dedicated to reading the Word of God every day. In this Lenten season, we will spend six weeks reading through the book of Isaiah, along with complementary passages of Scripture, to hear God's message of repentance and redemption through His messenger, Isaiah. We will then turn to a set of Holy Week readings for the final week of this plan, following the story of Jesus's last week before His death and resurrection.

READ & REFLECT

Your **He Will Save Us: A Lenten Study of Isaiah** book focuses primarily on Scripture, with added features to come alongside your time with God's Word.

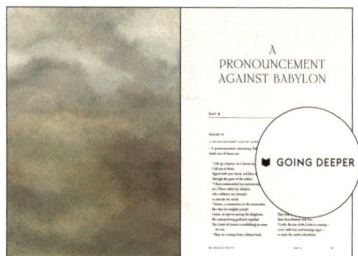

SCRIPTURE READING

Designed for a Monday start, this book presents the book of Isaiah in daily readings, along with additional passages curated to show how themes from the main reading can be found throughout Scripture. The last week of reading focuses on Holy Week.

Additional passages are marked in your daily reading with the Going Deeper heading.

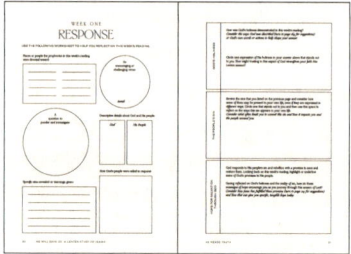

WORKSHEETS

Each week features an interactive worksheet.

COMMUNITY & CONVERSATION

You can start reading this book at any time. If you want to join men from across the globe as they read along with you, the He Reads Truth community will start Day 1 of **He Will Save Us: A Lenten Study of Isaiah** on Monday, March 3, 2025.

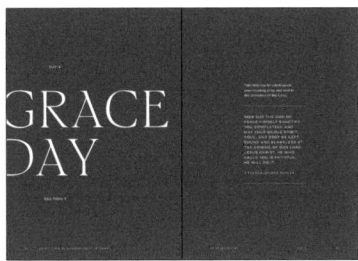

GRACE DAY

Use Saturdays to catch up on your reading, pray, and rest in the presence of the Lord.

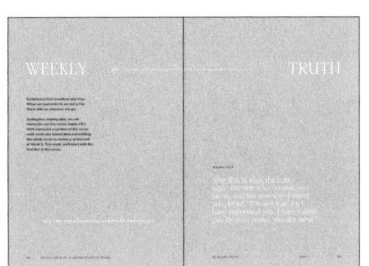

WEEKLY TRUTH

Sundays are set aside for Scripture memorization.

See tips for memorizing Scripture on page 272.

EXTRAS

This book features additional tools to help you gain a deeper understanding of the text.

Find a complete list of extras on pages 10–13.

 HE READS TRUTH APP

Devotionals corresponding to each daily reading can be found in the **Lent 2025: He Will Save Us** reading plan on the He Reads Truth app. New devotionals will be published each weekday once the plan begins on Monday, March 3, 2025. You can use the app to participate in community discussion and more.

 HEREADSTRUTH.COM

The **Lent 2025: He Will Save Us** reading plan and devotionals will also be available at HeReadsTruth.com as the community reads each day. Invite your family, friends, and neighbors to read along with you.

TABLE OF CONTENTS

EXTRA	Introduction: Isaiah	14
EXTRA	Tips for Reading Prophets and Prophecy	18

SECTION ONE
Judgment and Justice

DAY 1	Judah on Trial	22
DAY 2	Judah's Sins Denounced	29
EXTRA	Lent and the Church Calendar	34
DAY 3	Isaiah's Call	36
DAY 4	The Prince of Peace	40
DAY 5	The Reign of the Davidic King	46
WEEK ONE RESPONSE		50
DAY 6	Grace Day	52
DAY 7	Weekly Truth	54
DAY 8	A Pronouncement Against Babylon	57

DAY 9	A Pronouncement Concerning Moab	62
DAY 10	Judgment Against Israel	66
DAY 11	A Pronouncement Against Egypt	70
DAY 12	A Pronouncement Against Jerusalem	76
WEEK TWO RESPONSE		80
DAY 13	Grace Day	82
DAY 14	Weekly Truth	84
DAY 15	Salvation and Judgment	86
HYMN	Come, Thou Almighty King	92
DAY 16	The Song of Judah	95
DAY 17	The Lord's Vineyard	98
DAY 18	The Lord's Mercy to Israel	104
DAY 19	The Righteous Kingdom Announced	110
WEEK THREE RESPONSE		114
DAY 20	Grace Day	116
DAY 21	Weekly Truth	118
DAY 22	The Lord Rises Up	120
DAY 23	The Ransomed Return	127
DAY 24	Hezekiah's Prayer	132

SECTION TWO
Salvation and Solace

DAY 25	God's People Comforted	140
DAY 26	The Servant's Mission	146
WEEK FOUR RESPONSE		152
DAY 27	Grace Day	154
DAY 28	Weekly Truth	156
DAY 29	God Alone Is the Savior	158
EXTRA	Names for God in Isaiah	164
DAY 30	The Servant Brings Salvation	166
DAY 31	Salvation for Zion	172
DAY 32	The Servant's Suffering and Exaltation	178
HYMN	Hallelujah, What a Savior!	182
DAY 33	Come to the Lord	185
WEEK FIVE RESPONSE		190
DAY 34	Grace Day	192
DAY 35	Weekly Truth	194

SECTION THREE

Repentance and Restoration

DAY 36	Healing and Peace	198
DAY 37	The Lord's Glory in Zion	204
DAY 38	Zion's Restoration	211
EXTRA	Prophecies from Isaiah Fulfilled in Jesus	214
DAY 39	Israel's Prayer	218
DAY 40	Joyous Restoration	224
WEEK SIX RESPONSE		230
DAY 41	Grace Day	232

SECTION FOUR

Holy Week

DAY 42	Palm Sunday	237
DAY 43	Jesus Cleanses the Temple	240
DAY 44	Jesus Teaches in the Temple	244
DAY 45	Jesus Is Anointed for Burial	248
DAY 46	The Last Supper	250
DAY 47	Good Friday	256
HYMN	When I Survey the Wondrous Cross	260
DAY 48	Holy Saturday	262
DAY 49	Easter Sunday	266
EXTRA	For the Record	276

INTRODUCTION
ISAIAH

TIME TO READ ISAIAH: 3 HOURS, 43 MINUTES

KEY VERSE

Now this is what the LORD says—the one who created you, Jacob, and the one who formed you, Israel—"Do not fear, for I have redeemed you; I have called you by your name; you are mine."

–Isaiah 43:1

ON THE TIMELINE

Isaiah 6:1 records that Isaiah received his prophetic call in the last year of Uzziah's reign over Judah, about 740 BC. The superscription—an introductory element common to books of prophecy—in Isaiah 1:1 dates Isaiah's prophetic activity as covering all or part of the reigns of four kings of Judah: Uzziah, Jotham, Ahaz, and Hezekiah. Isaiah's prophetic ministry concluded sometime around the northern kingdom's exile into Assyria in 722 BC.

931 BC

Israel's division into two kingdoms, Israel (northern) and Judah (southern)

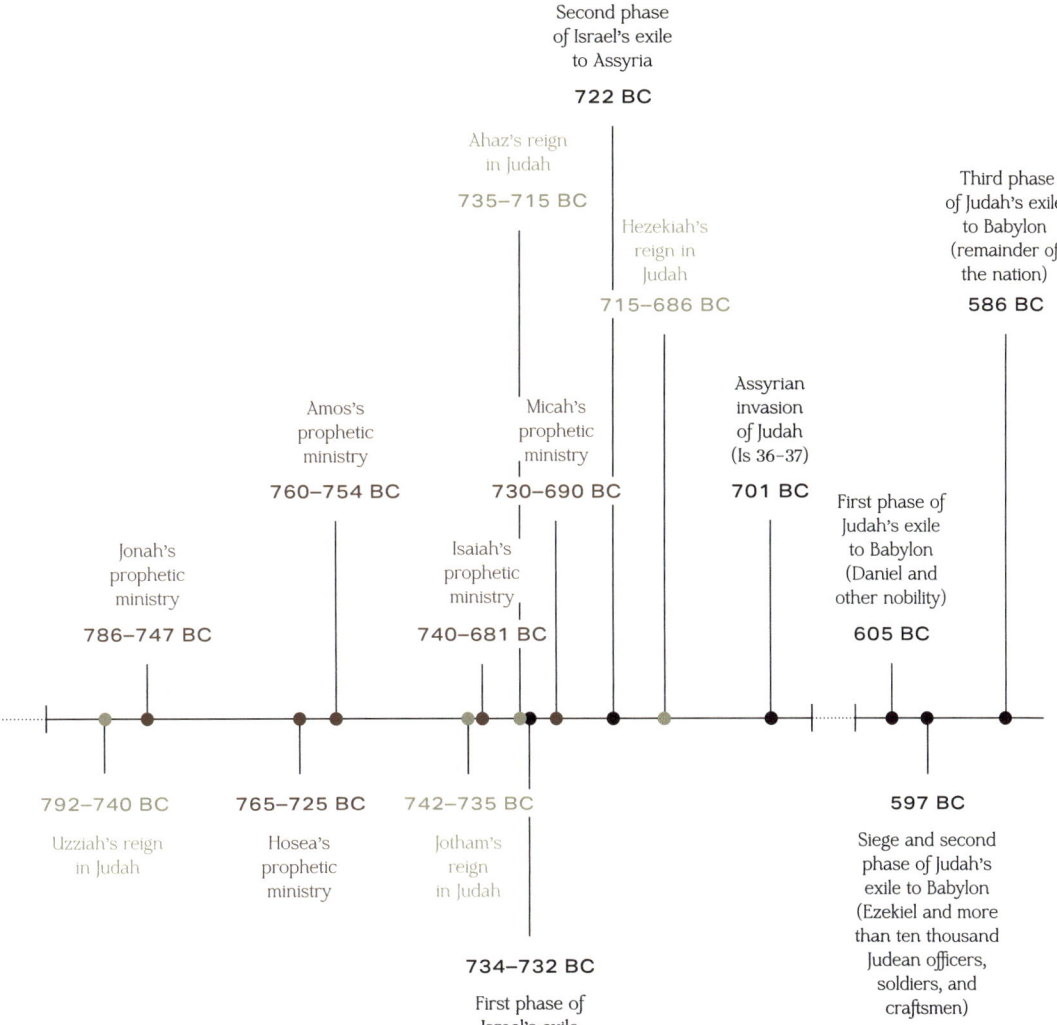

- **A LITTLE BACKGROUND**

- **MESSAGE & PURPOSE**

- **INTERESTING FACTS ABOUT ISAIAH**

The book of Isaiah presents itself as the writing of Isaiah, son of Amoz. Not much is known about Isaiah apart from his prophecy, but he was married to a woman referred to as "the prophetess" (Is 8:3), and together they had two sons. Isaiah ministered specifically to the southern kingdom of Judah. The events Isaiah prophesied about extended beyond the eighth century BC, through the rest of the Old Testament period, and beyond. The New Testament authors cited prophecies from Isaiah as finding fulfillment in the events surrounding Jesus Christ.

Isaiah's purpose was to call Judah away from the idolatry and sin that was poisoning their nation, urging them to remember both God's wrath toward rebellion and the goodness of walking in the ways of the Lord. While God would use foreign invaders to accomplish His purpose and bring judgment to the people, Isaiah encouraged them with their hope in God, the One who would extend mercy and fully redeem their transgressions.

Isaiah's message to the nation of Judah consists of a few key themes:
- Judgment and justice (Is 1–39)
- Salvation and solace (Is 40–55)
- Repentance and restoration (Is 56–66)

- Isaiah's name means "The Lord Saves," a fitting summary of his prophetic message.

- Some of Isaiah's contemporaries were the prophets Jonah, Amos, Hosea, and Micah.

- The word *salvation* appears nearly thirty times in the book of Isaiah but only about ten times in all other prophetic books combined.

- Isaiah is mentioned by name over twenty times in the Old Testament. He is also quoted over sixty-five times in the New Testament—more than any other prophet.

- **GIVE THANKS FOR THE BOOK OF ISAIAH**

The book of Isaiah details the consequences and sorrow of turning from God and choosing lesser things. It also shows us the God who does not let His people stay stuck in sin and rebellion forever. A full reading of Isaiah enriches our understanding of how these Old Testament prophecies are indeed fulfilled in Jesus Christ.

We are grateful for Isaiah's urgent reminder that our sin destroys and harms us and it is not worth the cost. More than that, we give thanks for the God who cares enough about His people to send the promised Messiah to ensure all people have a way to a restored relationship with Him.

- **ISAIAH FOR LENT**

The season of Lent provides an opportunity for Christians to reflect on their desperate need for salvation through the lens of the cross and the empty tomb (see "Lent and the Church Calendar" on page 34 for more). The book of Isaiah mirrors these Lenten rhythms as the prophet called the people of Judah to reflect on their own idolatry, injustice, and brokenness.

As believers today, the book of Isaiah reminds us to fully acknowledge the depth of our own sin. And it's in the book of Isaiah that we read about the prophesied Savior who would come to bring forgiveness and restoration. From the people of Judah to believers today, the book of Isaiah urges us to find hope in this truth: He will save us.

TIPS FOR READING PROPHETS AND PROPHECY

1

IN ORDER TO DISCERN THE MEANING OF THESE MESSAGES, WE SHOULD FIRST UNDERSTAND THEM IN THEIR ORIGINAL SETTING.

The prophets delivered God's messages to Israel, Judah, and other ancient Near Eastern cultures using relevant historical, geographical, political, and cultural context.

2

OLD TESTAMENT PROPHECY IS RELATIONAL.

Although the prophetic books often deal with concepts like famine, displacement, and God's judgment, the existence of these books shows that God deals with His people and other nations in the context of relationship.

3

PROPHETIC BOOKS REFLECT ON THE STORY OF GOD'S PEOPLE.

As the prophets in the Old Testament preached to God's people, they were drawing on the terms and themes of the Mosaic covenant at specific moments in Israel's and Judah's histories. Many prophets shared a similar three-part message:

- *You have broken God's covenant, and you must repent.*
- *If you do not humble yourselves before God, He will judge your actions.*
- *Even if He brings judgment, He will bring a future restoration.*

4
BOOKS OF PROPHECY ARE COLLECTIONS OF ALLEGORIES, PARABLES, PROSE, SERMONS, ORACLES, PRAYERS, POETRY, AND SHORT NARRATIVE EPISODES.

While they are organized into sections and categories, books of prophecy should not be taken as collectively chronological or plot driven (as narrative literature is). These works frequently include literary devices to communicate truth. For example, the book of Isaiah uses personification (Is 55:12), wordplay (Is 5:7), rhetorical questions (Is 40:12–14, 18; 44:19), metaphor (Is 1:21; 40:6–8), irony (Is 52:13–15), simile (Is 1:18), and other literary techniques for emphasis.

5
EACH PROPHETIC BOOK HAS UNIQUE THEMES AND SYMBOLS.

The prophets each delivered God's message, but their contexts, personalities, and emphases varied. Isaiah includes themes of a new exodus (Is 40–55), the suffering servant (Is 52:13–53:12), and God as the Holy One of Israel (Is 12:6). Isaiah also included many prophecies about the Messiah (Is 7:14; 9:1–7; 11:1–5; 53:1–12).

6
GOD'S ATTRIBUTES ARE WHOLLY PRESENT THROUGHOUT EVERY ONE OF HIS MESSAGES.

God is not sometimes loving and sometimes holy, or sometimes righteous and sometimes good. God is all of His attributes all of the time. Though the unique attributes can be identified individually to aid in our own comprehension, His essence remains undivided. When reading passages that more clearly reveal one attribute over another, remember that all other attributes of God remain true.

7
THE DARKER PROPHECY GETS, THE BRIGHTER THE CROSS APPEARS.

The bleak imagery of the Old Testament prophets shows the seriousness of sin and the reality that we do not have hope without a redeemer. And in the New Testament, we see a Savior who went to the cross to atone for these dark realities described in the prophetic books, was resurrected to bring victory over death, and ascended to reign over creation for eternity.

SECTION ONE

JUDGMENT AND JUSTICE

ISAIAH 1–39

Isaiah 1–39 describes a tumultuous time in Judah's history. Foreign powers encroached their borders, power dynamics stirred tension amongst Judah's leadership, and God's people turned to the false gods of the surrounding nations for answers. In the middle of this upheaval, Isaiah was sent with a message of judgment for Judah's unrighteousness: God's people sinned and rebelled against the One who made and rescued them, and God promised justice to those who had been wronged.

Isaiah's message was an urgent warning for the nation to return to God's ways and avoid His discipline, but it is also a telling of the inevitable consequences that would come because of the injustices Judah has already committed. God is merciful and compassionate, and **He also stands against the evil that oppresses the powerless and the idolatry that steals His people away from glorifying the one true God**. This juxtaposition is seen throughout these chapters, most notably in chapter 11's image of a king who would come from the line of David and bring about God's will and kingdom. This King would bring judgment that heals, justice that restores, and peace to the land.

JUDAH ON TRIAL

THEY HAVE ABANDONED THE LORD;
THEY HAVE DESPISED THE HOLY ONE
OF ISRAEL; THEY HAVE TURNED THEIR
BACKS ON HIM.

ISAIAH 1:4

DAY 1   SECTION 1

ISAIAH 1

¹ The vision concerning Judah and Jerusalem that Isaiah son of Amoz saw during the reigns of Kings Uzziah, Jotham, Ahaz, and Hezekiah of Judah.

JUDAH ON TRIAL

² Listen, heavens, and pay attention, earth,
for the Lord has spoken:
"I have raised children and brought them up,
but they have rebelled against me.
³ The ox knows its owner,
and the donkey its master's feeding trough,
but Israel does not know;
my people do not understand."

⁴ Oh sinful nation,
people weighed down with iniquity,
brood of evildoers,
depraved children!
They have abandoned the Lord;
they have despised the Holy One of Israel;
they have turned their backs on him.

⁵ Why do you want more beatings?
Why do you keep on rebelling?
The whole head is hurt,
and the whole heart is sick.
⁶ From the sole of the foot even to the head,
no spot is uninjured—
wounds, welts, and festering sores
not cleansed, bandaged,
or soothed with oil.

⁷ Your land is desolate,
your cities burned down;
foreigners devour your fields
right in front of you—
a desolation, like a place demolished by foreigners.
⁸ Daughter Zion is abandoned
like a shelter in a vineyard,

like a shack in a cucumber field,
like a besieged city.
⁹ If the LORD of Armies
had not left us a few survivors,
we would be like Sodom,
we would resemble Gomorrah.

¹⁰ Hear the word of the LORD,
you rulers of Sodom!
Listen to the instruction of our God,
you people of Gomorrah!
¹¹ "What are all your sacrifices to me?"
asks the LORD.
"I have had enough of burnt offerings
    and rams
and the fat of well-fed cattle;
I have no desire for the blood of bulls,
lambs, or male goats.
¹² When you come to appear before me,
who requires this from you—
this trampling of my courts?
¹³ Stop bringing useless offerings.
Your incense is detestable to me.
New Moons and Sabbaths,
and the calling of solemn assemblies—
I cannot stand iniquity with a festival.
¹⁴ I hate your New Moons and
    prescribed festivals.
They have become a burden to me;
I am tired of putting up with them.
¹⁵ When you spread out your hands in prayer,
I will refuse to look at you;
even if you offer countless prayers,
I will not listen.
Your hands are covered with blood.

PURIFICATION OF JERUSALEM

¹⁶ "Wash yourselves. Cleanse yourselves.
Remove your evil deeds from my sight.
Stop doing evil.
¹⁷ Learn to do what is good.
Pursue justice.
Correct the oppressor.
Defend the rights of the fatherless.
Plead the widow's cause.

¹⁸ "Come, let's settle this,"
says the LORD.
"Though your sins are scarlet,
they will be as white as snow;
though they are crimson red,
they will be like wool.
¹⁹ If you are willing and obedient,
you will eat the good things of the land.
²⁰ But if you refuse and rebel,
you will be devoured by the sword."
For the mouth of the LORD has spoken.

²¹ The faithful town—
what an adulteress she has become!
She was once full of justice.
Righteousness once dwelt in her,
but now, murderers!
²² Your silver has become dross to
    be discarded,
your beer is diluted with water.
²³ Your rulers are rebels,
friends of thieves.
They all love graft
and chase after bribes.
They do not defend the rights of
    the fatherless,
and the widow's case never comes
    before them.

²⁴ Therefore the Lord GOD of Armies,
the Mighty One of Israel, declares:
"Ah, I will get even with my foes;
I will take revenge against my enemies.
²⁵ I will turn my hand against you

and will burn away your dross completely;
I will remove all your impurities.
²⁶ I will restore your judges to what they were at first,
and your advisers to what they were at the start.
Afterward you will be called the Righteous City,
a Faithful Town."

²⁷ Zion will be redeemed by justice,
those who repent, by righteousness.
²⁸ At the same time both rebels and sinners will be broken,
and those who abandon the LORD will perish.
²⁹ Indeed, they will be ashamed of the sacred trees
you desired,
and you will be embarrassed because of the garden shrines
you have chosen.
³⁰ For you will become like an oak
whose leaves are withered,
and like a garden without water.
³¹ The strong one will become tinder,
and his work a spark;
both will burn together,
with no one to extinguish the flames.

ISAIAH 2

THE CITY OF PEACE

¹ The vision that Isaiah son of Amoz saw concerning Judah and Jerusalem:

² In the last days
the mountain of the LORD's house will be established
at the top of the mountains
and will be raised above the hills.
All nations will stream to it,
³ and many peoples will come and say,
"Come, let's go up to the mountain of the LORD,
to the house of the God of Jacob.
He will teach us about his ways
so that we may walk in his paths."
For instruction will go out of Zion
and the word of the LORD from Jerusalem.

NOTES

⁴ He will settle disputes among the nations
and provide arbitration for many peoples.
They will beat their swords into plows
and their spears into pruning knives.
Nation will not take up the sword against nation,
and they will never again train for war.

THE DAY OF THE LORD

⁵ House of Jacob,
come and let's walk in the Lord's light.
⁶ For you have abandoned your people,
the house of Jacob,
because they are full of divination from the East
and of fortune-tellers like the Philistines.
They are in league with foreigners.
⁷ Their land is full of silver and gold,
and there is no limit to their treasures;
their land is full of horses,
and there is no limit to their chariots.
⁸ Their land is full of worthless idols;
they worship the work of their hands,
what their fingers have made.
⁹ So humanity is brought low,
and each person is humbled.
Do not forgive them!
¹⁰ Go into the rocks
and hide in the dust
from the terror of the Lord
and from his majestic splendor.
¹¹ The pride of mankind will be humbled,
and human loftiness will be brought low;
the Lord alone will be exalted on that day.

¹² For a day belonging to the Lord of Armies is coming
against all that is proud and lofty,
against all that is lifted up—it will be humbled—
¹³ against all the cedars of Lebanon,
lofty and lifted up,
against all the oaks of Bashan,
¹⁴ against all the high mountains,
against all the lofty hills,

¹⁵ against every high tower,
and against every fortified wall,
¹⁶ against every ship of Tarshish,
and against every splendid sea vessel.
¹⁷ The pride of mankind will be brought low,
and human loftiness will be humbled;
the Lord alone will be exalted on that day.
¹⁸ The worthless idols will vanish completely.

¹⁹ People will go into caves in the rocks
and holes in the ground,
away from the terror of the Lord
and from his majestic splendor,
when he rises to terrify the earth.
²⁰ On that day people will throw
their worthless idols of silver and gold,
which they made to worship,
to the moles and the bats.
²¹ They will go into the caves of the rocks
and the crevices in the cliffs,
away from the terror of the Lord
and from his majestic splendor,
when he rises to terrify the earth.
²² Put no more trust in a mere human,
who has only the breath in his nostrils.
What is he really worth?

◼ GOING DEEPER

DEUTERONOMY 11:26-28

A BLESSING AND A CURSE

²⁶ Look, today I set before you a blessing and a curse:

²⁷ there will be a blessing, if you obey the commands of the Lord your God I am giving you today,

²⁸ and a curse, if you do not obey the commands of the Lord your God and you turn aside from the path I command you today by following other gods you have not known.

JUDAH'S SINS DENOUNCED

DAY 2 SECTION 1

ISAIAH 3

JUDAH'S LEADERS JUDGED

¹ Note this: The Lord God of Armies
is about to remove from Jerusalem and
    from Judah
every kind of security:
the entire supply of bread and water,
² heroes and warriors,
judges and prophets,
fortune-tellers and elders,
³ commanders of fifty and dignitaries,
counselors, cunning magicians,
    and necromancers.
⁴ "I will make youths their leaders,
and unstable rulers will govern them."
⁵ The people will oppress one another,
man against man, neighbor against neighbor;
the young will act arrogantly toward the old,
and the worthless toward the honorable.
⁶ A man will even seize his brother
in his father's house, saying,
"You have a cloak—you be our leader!
This heap of rubble will be under
    your control."
⁷ On that day he will cry out, saying,
"I'm not a healer.
I don't even have food or clothing in
    my house.
Don't make me the leader of the people!"
⁸ For Jerusalem has stumbled
and Judah has fallen
because they have spoken and acted against
    the Lord,
defying his glorious presence.
⁹ The look on their faces testifies
    against them,
and like Sodom, they flaunt their sin;
they do not conceal it.
Woe to them,
for they have brought disaster on themselves.
¹⁰ Tell the righteous that it will go well
    for them,

for they will eat the fruit of their labor.
¹¹ Woe to the wicked—it will go badly
    for them,
for what they have done will be done
    to them.
¹² Youths oppress my people,
and women rule over them.
My people, your leaders mislead you;
they confuse the direction of your paths.

¹³ The Lord rises to argue the case
and stands to judge the people.
¹⁴ The Lord brings this charge
against the elders and leaders of his people:
"You have devastated the vineyard.
The plunder from the poor is in your houses.
¹⁵ Why do you crush my people
and grind the faces of the poor?"
    This is the declaration of the Lord God
        of Armies.

JERUSALEM'S WOMEN JUDGED

¹⁶ The Lord also says:

Because the daughters of Zion are haughty,
walking with heads held high
and seductive eyes,
prancing along,
jingling their ankle bracelets,
¹⁷ the Lord will put scabs on the heads
of the daughters of Zion,
and the Lord will shave their foreheads bare.

¹⁸ On that day the Lord will strip their finery: ankle bracelets, headbands, crescents, ¹⁹ pendants, bracelets, veils, ²⁰ headdresses, ankle jewelry, sashes, perfume bottles, amulets, ²¹ signet rings, nose rings, ²² festive robes, capes, cloaks, purses, ²³ garments, linen clothes, turbans, and shawls.

²⁴ Instead of perfume there will be a stench;
instead of a belt, a rope;
instead of beautifully styled hair, baldness;
instead of fine clothes, sackcloth;
instead of beauty, branding.
²⁵ Your men will fall by the sword,
your warriors in battle.
²⁶ Then her gates will lament and mourn;
deserted, she will sit on the ground.

ISAIAH 4

¹ On that day seven women
will seize one man, saying,
"We will eat our own bread
and provide our own clothing.
Just let us bear your name.
Take away our disgrace."

ZION'S FUTURE GLORY

² On that day the Branch of the Lord will be beautiful and glorious, and the fruit of the land will be the pride and glory of Israel's survivors. ³ Whoever remains in Zion and whoever is left in Jerusalem will be called holy—all in Jerusalem written in the book of life— ⁴ when the Lord has washed away the filth of the daughters of Zion and cleansed the bloodguilt from the heart of Jerusalem by a spirit of judgment and a spirit of burning. ⁵ Then the Lord will create a cloud of smoke by day and a glowing flame of fire by night over the entire site of Mount Zion and over its assemblies. For there will be a canopy over all the glory, ⁶ and there will be a shelter for shade from heat by day and a refuge and shelter from storm and rain.

ISAIAH 5

SONG OF THE VINEYARD

¹ I will sing about the one I love,
a song about my loved one's vineyard:
The one I love had a vineyard

on a very fertile hill.
² He broke up the soil, cleared it of stones,
and planted it with the finest vines.
He built a tower in the middle of it
and even dug out a winepress there.
He expected it to yield good grapes,
but it yielded worthless grapes.

³ So now, residents of Jerusalem
and men of Judah,
please judge between me
and my vineyard.
⁴ What more could I have done for my vineyard
than I did?
Why, when I expected a yield of good grapes,
did it yield worthless grapes?
⁵ Now I will tell you
what I am about to do to my vineyard:
I will remove its hedge,
and it will be consumed;
I will tear down its wall,
and it will be trampled.
⁶ I will make it a wasteland.
It will not be pruned or weeded;
thorns and briers will grow up.
I will also give orders to the clouds
that rain should not fall on it.
⁷ For the vineyard of the Lord of Armies
is the house of Israel,
and the men of Judah,
the plant he delighted in.
He expected justice
but saw injustice;
he expected righteousness
but heard cries of despair.

JUDAH'S SINS DENOUNCED

⁸ Woe to those who add house to house
and join field to field
until there is no more room
and you alone are left in the land.

NOTES

⁹ I heard the Lord of Armies say:

Indeed, many houses will become desolate,
grand and lovely ones without inhabitants.
¹⁰ For a ten-acre vineyard will yield
only six gallons of wine,
and ten bushels of seed will yield
only one bushel of grain.

¹¹ Woe to those who rise early in the morning
in pursuit of beer,
who linger into the evening,
inflamed by wine.
¹² At their feasts they have lyre, harp,
tambourine, flute, and wine.
They do not perceive the Lord's actions,
and they do not see the work of his hands.

¹³ Therefore my people will go into exile
because they lack knowledge;
her dignitaries are starving,
and her masses are parched with thirst.
¹⁴ Therefore Sheol enlarges its throat
and opens wide its enormous jaws,
and down go Zion's dignitaries, her masses,
her crowds, and those who celebrate in her!
¹⁵ Humanity is brought low, each person
  is humbled,
and haughty eyes are humbled.
¹⁶ But the Lord of Armies is exalted by
  his justice,
and the holy God demonstrates his holiness
through his righteousness.
¹⁷ Lambs will graze
as if in their own pastures,
and resident aliens will eat
among the ruins of the rich.

¹⁸ Woe to those who drag iniquity
with cords of deceit
and pull sin along with cart ropes,
¹⁹ to those who say,
"Let him hurry up and do his work quickly
so that we can see it!
Let the plan of the Holy One of Israel
  take place
so that we can know it!"
²⁰ Woe to those who call evil good
and good evil,
who substitute darkness for light
and light for darkness,
who substitute bitter for sweet
and sweet for bitter.
²¹ Woe to those who consider
  themselves wise
and judge themselves clever.
²² Woe to those who are heroes at
  drinking wine,
who are champions at pouring beer,
²³ who acquit the guilty for a bribe
and deprive the innocent of justice.

²⁴ Therefore, as a tongue of fire
  consumes straw
and as dry grass shrivels in the flame,
so their roots will become like
  something rotten
and their blossoms will blow away
  like dust,
for they have rejected
the instruction of the Lord of Armies,
and they have despised
the word of the Holy One of Israel.
²⁵ Therefore the Lord's anger burned against
  his people.
He raised his hand against them and
  struck them;
the mountains quaked,
and their corpses were like garbage in
  the streets.
In all this, his anger has not turned away,
and his hand is still raised to strike.

²⁶ He raises a signal flag for the distant nations
and whistles for them from the ends of the earth.
Look—how quickly and swiftly they come!
²⁷ None of them grows weary or stumbles;
no one slumbers or sleeps.
No belt is loose
and no sandal strap broken.
²⁸ Their arrows are sharpened,
and all their bows strung.
Their horses' hooves are like flint;
their chariot wheels are like a whirlwind.
²⁹ Their roaring is like a lion's;
they roar like young lions;
they growl and seize their prey
and carry it off,
and no one can rescue it.
³⁰ On that day they will roar over it,
like the roaring of the sea.
When one looks at the land,
there will be darkness and distress;
light will be obscured by clouds.

GOING DEEPER

MATTHEW 18:6-9

⁶ "But whoever causes one of these little ones who believe in me to fall away—it would be better for him if a heavy millstone were hung around his neck and he were drowned in the depths of the sea. ⁷ Woe to the world because of offenses. For offenses will inevitably come, but woe to that person by whom the offense comes. ⁸ If your hand or your foot causes you to fall away, cut it off and throw it away. It is better for you to enter life maimed or lame than to have two hands or two feet and be thrown into the eternal fire. ⁹ And if your eye causes you to fall away, gouge it out and throw it away. It is better for you to enter life with one eye than to have two eyes and be thrown into hellfire."

LENT AND THE CHURCH CALENDAR

The season of Lent is just one part of the Church calendar, a centuries-old way many Christian denominations order the year to regularly remember and celebrate the redeeming work of Christ. Lent is a solemn season of self-reflection, repentance, and Scripture meditation as a means of preparing to celebrate Easter.

Lent invites us to remember some of the more uncomfortable realities of our lives that God has redeemed through Jesus. Just as the first humans rebelled against God (Gn 3:1-7), we, too, have turned away from Him and, along with creation, are subject to the death, decay, and frustration that comes from sin (Rm 8:20-21). Through His Son, God offers forgiveness of sins, and by His Holy Spirit, He actively forms us into the image of Christ (Rm 8:9-11). Lent allows us to reflect on this redemption narrative, recognizing our need for forgiveness and our opportunity to rejoice in what God has done in Jesus.

Structured around the moving date of Easter Sunday and the fixed date of Christmas, the liturgical Church calendar consists of six seasons as well as ordinary time. Listed here are the three seasons corresponding to Lent and Easter.

LENT

WHEN IS IT? — Lent begins on Ash Wednesday and continues through Holy Saturday, a period of forty fasting days and six feasting Sundays.

KEY SCRIPTURE: — Lk 4:1-13

EASTERTIDE

WHEN IS IT? — Beginning on Easter Sunday, this season goes until the day before Pentecost. At seven weeks, it is the longest formal season of the Church year.

KEY SCRIPTURES: — Lk 24:1-12, 36-53; Jn 11:25-26

PENTECOST

WHEN IS IT? — Pentecost is the seventh Sunday after Easter.

KEY SCRIPTURE: — Ac 2:1-41

ISAIAH'S CALL

DAY 3   **SECTION 1**

ISAIAH 6

ISAIAH'S CALL AND MISSION

¹ In the year that King Uzziah died, I saw the Lord seated on a high and lofty throne, and the hem of his robe filled the temple. ² Seraphim were standing above him; they each had six wings: with two they covered their faces, with two they covered their feet, and with two they flew. ³ And one called to another:

> Holy, holy, holy is the Lord of Armies;
> his glory fills the whole earth.

⁴ The foundations of the doorways shook at the sound of their voices, and the temple was filled with smoke.

⁵ Then I said:

> Woe is me for I am ruined
> because I am a man of unclean lips
> and live among a people of unclean lips,
> and because my eyes have seen the King,
> the Lord of Armies.

⁶ Then one of the seraphim flew to me, and in his hand was a glowing coal that he had taken from the altar with tongs. ⁷ He touched my mouth with it and said:

> Now that this has touched your lips,
> your iniquity is removed
> and your sin is atoned for.

⁸ Then I heard the voice of the Lord asking:

> Who will I send?
> Who will go for us?

I said:

Here I am. Send me.

⁹ And he replied:

> Go! Say to these people:
> Keep listening, but do not understand;
> keep looking, but do not perceive.
> ¹⁰ Make the minds of these people dull;
> deafen their ears and blind their eyes;
> otherwise they might see with their eyes
> and hear with their ears,
> understand with their minds,
> turn back, and be healed.

¹¹ Then I said, "Until when, Lord?" And he replied:

Until cities lie in ruins without inhabitants,
houses are without people,
the land is ruined and desolate,
¹² and the LORD drives the people far away,
leaving great emptiness in the land.
¹³ Though a tenth will remain in the land,
it will be burned again.
Like the terebinth or the oak
that leaves a stump when felled,
the holy seed is the stump.

ISAIAH 7

THE MESSAGE TO AHAZ

¹ This took place during the reign of Ahaz, son of Jotham, son of Uzziah king of Judah: Aram's King Rezin and Israel's King Pekah son of Remaliah went to fight against Jerusalem, but they were not able to conquer it.

² When it became known to the house of David that Aram had occupied Ephraim, the heart of Ahaz and the hearts of his people trembled like trees of a forest shaking in the wind.

³ The LORD said to Isaiah, "Go out with your son Shear-jashub to meet Ahaz at the end of the conduit of the upper pool, by the road to the Launderer's Field. ⁴ Say to him: Calm down and be quiet. Don't be afraid or cowardly because of these two smoldering sticks, the fierce anger of Rezin and Aram, and the son of Remaliah. ⁵ For Aram, along with Ephraim and the son of Remaliah, has plotted harm against you. They say, ⁶ 'Let's go up against Judah, terrorize it, and conquer it for ourselves. Then we can install Tabeel's son as king in it.'"

⁷ This is what the Lord GOD says:

It will not happen; it will not occur.
⁸ The chief city of Aram is Damascus,
the chief of Damascus is Rezin
(within sixty-five years
Ephraim will be too shattered to be a people),
⁹ the chief city of Ephraim is Samaria,
and the chief of Samaria is the son of Remaliah.

If you do not stand firm in your faith,
then you will not stand at all.

THE IMMANUEL PROPHECY

¹⁰ Then the Lord spoke again to Ahaz: ¹¹ "Ask for a sign from the Lord your God—it can be as deep as Sheol or as high as heaven."

¹² But Ahaz replied, "I will not ask. I will not test the Lord."

¹³ Isaiah said, "Listen, house of David! Is it not enough for you to try the patience of men? Will you also try the patience of my God? ¹⁴ Therefore, the Lord himself will give you a sign: See, the virgin will conceive, have a son, and name him Immanuel. ¹⁵ By the time he learns to reject what is bad and choose what is good, he will be eating curds and honey. ¹⁶ For before the boy knows to reject what is bad and choose what is good, the land of the two kings you dread will be abandoned. ¹⁷ The Lord will bring on you, your people, and your father's house such a time as has never been since Ephraim separated from Judah: He will bring the king of Assyria."

¹⁸ On that day
the Lord will whistle to flies
at the farthest streams of the Nile
and to bees in the land of Assyria.
¹⁹ All of them will come and settle
in the steep ravines, in the clefts of the rocks,
in all the thornbushes, and in all the
water holes.

²⁰ On that day the Lord will use a razor hired from beyond the Euphrates River—the king of Assyria—to shave the hair on your heads, the hair on your legs, and even your beards.

²¹ On that day
a man will raise a young cow and two sheep,
²² and from the abundant milk they give
he will eat curds,
for every survivor in the land will eat curds
and honey.

²³ And on that day
every place where there were a
thousand vines,
worth a thousand pieces of silver,
will become thorns and briers.
²⁴ A man will go there with bow
and arrows
because the whole land will be thorns
and briers.
²⁵ You will not go to all the hills
that were once tilled with a hoe,
for fear of the thorns and briers.
Those hills will be places for oxen to graze
and for sheep to trample.

ISAIAH 8:1–10

THE COMING ASSYRIAN INVASION

¹ Then the Lord said to me, "Take a large piece of parchment and write on it with an ordinary pen: Maher-shalal-hash-baz. ² I have appointed trustworthy witnesses—the priest Uriah and Zechariah son of Jeberechiah."

³ I was then intimate with the prophetess, and she conceived and gave birth to a son. The Lord said to me, "Name him Maher-shalal-hash-baz, ⁴ for before the boy knows how to call

'Father,' or 'Mother,' the wealth of Damascus and the spoils of Samaria will be carried off to the king of Assyria."

⁵ The Lord spoke to me again:

⁶ Because these people rejected
the slowly flowing water of Shiloah
and rejoiced with Rezin
and the son of Remaliah,
⁷ the Lord will certainly bring against them
the mighty rushing water of the Euphrates River—
the king of Assyria and all his glory.
It will overflow its channels
and spill over all its banks.
⁸ It will pour into Judah,
flood over it, and sweep through,
reaching up to the neck;
and its flooded banks
will fill your entire land, Immanuel!

⁹ Band together, peoples, and be broken;
pay attention, all you distant lands;
prepare for war, and be broken;
prepare for war, and be broken.
¹⁰ Devise a plan; it will fail.
Make a prediction; it will not happen.
For God is with us.

◾ GOING DEEPER

1 THESSALONIANS 5:23-24

²³ Now may the God of peace himself sanctify you completely. And may your whole spirit, soul, and body be kept sound and blameless at the coming of our Lord Jesus Christ. ²⁴ He who calls you is faithful; he will do it.

DAY 4

THE PRINCE OF PEACE

SECTION 1

ISAIAH 8:11-22

THE LORD OF ARMIES, THE ONLY REFUGE

¹¹ For this is what the Lord said to me with great power, to keep me from going the way of this people:

¹² Do not call everything a conspiracy
that these people say is a conspiracy.
Do not fear what they fear;
do not be terrified.
¹³ You are to regard only the Lord of Armies as holy.
Only he should be feared;
only he should be held in awe.
¹⁴ He will be a sanctuary;
but for the two houses of Israel,
he will be a stone to stumble over
and a rock to trip over,
and a trap and a snare to the inhabitants of Jerusalem.
¹⁵ Many will stumble over these;
they will fall and be broken;
they will be snared and captured.

¹⁶ Bind up the testimony.
Seal up the instruction among my disciples.
¹⁷ I will wait for the Lord,
who is hiding his face from the house of Jacob.
I will wait for him.

¹⁸ Here I am with the children the Lord has given me to be signs and wonders in Israel from the Lord of Armies who dwells on Mount Zion. ¹⁹ When they say to you, "Inquire of the mediums and the spiritists who chirp and mutter," shouldn't a people inquire of their God? Should they inquire of the dead on behalf of the living? ²⁰ Go to God's instruction and testimony! If they do not speak according to this word, there will be no dawn for them.

²¹ They will wander through the land, dejected and hungry. When they are famished, they will become enraged, and, looking upward, will curse their king and their God. ²² They will look toward the earth and see only distress, darkness, and the gloom of affliction, and they will be driven into thick darkness.

ISAIAH 9

BIRTH OF THE PRINCE OF PEACE

¹ Nevertheless, the gloom of the distressed land will not be like that of the former times when he humbled the land of Zebulun and the land of Naphtali. But in the future he will bring honor to the way of the sea, to the land east of the Jordan, and to Galilee of the nations.

² The people walking in darkness
have seen a great light;
a light has dawned
on those living in the land of darkness.
³ You have enlarged the nation
and increased its joy.
The people have rejoiced before you
as they rejoice at harvest time
and as they rejoice when dividing spoils.
⁴ For you have shattered their
    oppressive yoke
and the rod on their shoulders,
the staff of their oppressor,
just as you did on the day of Midian.
⁵ For every trampling boot of battle
and the bloodied garments of war
will be burned as fuel for the fire.
⁶ For a child will be born for us,
a son will be given to us,
and the government will be on his shoulders.
He will be named
Wonderful Counselor, Mighty God,
Eternal Father, Prince of Peace.
⁷ The dominion will be vast,
and its prosperity will never end.
He will reign on the throne of David
and over his kingdom,
to establish and sustain it
with justice and righteousness from now on
    and forever.
The zeal of the Lord of Armies will
    accomplish this.

THE HAND RAISED AGAINST ISRAEL

⁸ The Lord sent a message against Jacob;
it came against Israel.
⁹ All the people—
Ephraim and the inhabitants of Samaria—
    will know it.
They will say with pride and arrogance,
¹⁰ "The bricks have fallen,
but we will rebuild with cut stones;
the sycamores have been cut down,
but we will replace them with cedars."
¹¹ The Lord has raised up Rezin's adversaries
    against him
and stirred up his enemies.
¹² Aram from the east and Philistia from
    the west
have consumed Israel with open mouths.
In all this, his anger has not turned away,
and his hand is still raised to strike.

¹³ The people did not turn to him who
    struck them;
they did not seek the Lord of Armies.
¹⁴ So the Lord cut off Israel's head and tail,
palm branch and reed in a single day.
¹⁵ The head is the elder, the honored one;
the tail is the prophet, the one teaching lies.
¹⁶ The leaders of the people mislead them,
and those they mislead are swallowed up.
¹⁷ Therefore the Lord does not rejoice
over Israel's young men
and has no compassion
on its fatherless and widows,
for everyone is a godless evildoer,
and every mouth speaks folly.
In all this, his anger has not turned away,
and his hand is still raised to strike.

¹⁸ For wickedness burns like a fire
that consumes thorns and briers

and kindles the forest thickets
so that they go up in a column of smoke.
¹⁹ The land is scorched
by the wrath of the LORD of Armies,
and the people are like fuel for the fire.
No one has compassion on his brother.
²⁰ They carve meat on the right,
but they are still hungry;
they have eaten on the left,
but they are still not satisfied.
Each one eats the flesh of his arm.
²¹ Manasseh eats Ephraim,
and Ephraim, Manasseh;
together, both are against Judah.
In all this, his anger has not turned away,
and his hand is still raised to strike.

ISAIAH 10:1–19

¹ Woe to those enacting crooked statutes
and writing oppressive laws
² to keep the poor from getting a fair trial
and to deprive the needy among my people of justice,
so that widows can be their spoil
and they can plunder the fatherless.
³ What will you do on the day of punishment
when devastation comes from far away?
Who will you run to for help?
Where will you leave your wealth?
⁴ There will be nothing to do
except crouch among the prisoners
or fall among the slain.
In all this, his anger has not turned away,
and his hand is still raised to strike.

ASSYRIA, THE INSTRUMENT OF WRATH

⁵ Woe to Assyria, the rod of my anger—
the staff in their hands is my wrath.
⁶ I will send him against a godless nation;
I will command him to go
against a people destined for my rage,

to take spoils, to plunder,
and to trample them down like clay in the streets.
⁷ But this is not what he intends;
this is not what he plans.
It is his intent to destroy
and to cut off many nations.
⁸ For he says,
"Aren't all my commanders kings?
⁹ Isn't Calno like Carchemish?
Isn't Hamath like Arpad?
Isn't Samaria like Damascus?
¹⁰ As my hand seized the kingdoms of worthless images,
kingdoms whose idols exceeded those of Jerusalem and Samaria,
¹¹ and as I did to Samaria and its worthless images
will I not also do to Jerusalem and its idols?"

JUDGMENT ON ASSYRIA

¹² But when the Lord finishes all his work against Mount Zion and Jerusalem, he will say, "I will punish the king of Assyria for his arrogant acts and the proud look in his eyes." ¹³ For he said:

I have done this by my own strength
and wisdom, for I am clever.
I abolished the borders of nations
and plundered their treasures;
like a mighty warrior, I subjugated the inhabitants.
¹⁴ My hand has reached out, as if into a nest,
to seize the wealth of the nations.
Like one gathering abandoned eggs,
I gathered the whole earth.
No wing fluttered;
no beak opened or chirped.

¹⁵ Does an ax exalt itself
above the one who chops with it?
Does a saw magnify itself
above the one who saws with it?
It would be like a rod waving the ones who lift it!
It would be like a staff lifting the one who isn't wood!

¹⁶ Therefore the Lord God of Armies
will inflict an emaciating disease
on the well-fed of Assyria,
and he will kindle a burning fire
under its glory.
¹⁷ Israel's Light will become a fire,
and its Holy One, a flame.
In one day it will burn and consume Assyria's thorns and thistles.
¹⁸ He will completely destroy
the glory of its forests and orchards
as a sickness consumes a person.
¹⁹ The remaining trees of its forest
will be so few in number
that a child could count them.

GOING DEEPER

MATTHEW 4:12-17

MINISTRY IN GALILEE

¹² When he heard that John had been arrested, he withdrew into Galilee. ¹³ He left Nazareth and went to live in Capernaum by the sea, in the region of Zebulun and Naphtali. ¹⁴ This was to fulfill what was spoken through the prophet Isaiah:

¹⁵ Land of Zebulun and land of Naphtali,
along the road by the sea, beyond the Jordan,
Galilee of the Gentiles.
¹⁶ The people who live in darkness
have seen a great light,
and for those living in the land of the shadow of death,
a light has dawned.

¹⁷ From then on Jesus began to preach, "Repent, because the kingdom of heaven has come near."

DAY 5   SECTION 1

THE REIGN OF THE DAVIDIC KING

ISAIAH 10:20–34

THE REMNANT WILL RETURN

²⁰ On that day the remnant of Israel and the survivors of the house of Jacob will no longer depend on the one who struck them, but they will faithfully depend on the LORD, the Holy One of Israel.

²¹ The remnant will return, the remnant of Jacob,
to the Mighty God.
²² Israel, even if your people were as numerous
as the sand of the sea,
only a remnant of them will return.
Destruction has been decreed;
justice overflows.
²³ For throughout the land
the Lord GOD of Armies
is carrying out a destruction that was decreed.

²⁴ Therefore, the Lord GOD of Armies says this: "My people who dwell in Zion, do not fear Assyria, though they strike you with a rod and raise their staff over you as the Egyptians did. ²⁵ In just a little while my wrath will be spent and my anger will turn to their destruction." ²⁶ And the LORD of Armies will

brandish a whip against him as he did when he struck Midian at the rock
of Oreb; and he will raise his staff over the sea as he did in Egypt.

GOD WILL JUDGE ASSYRIA

²⁷ On that day
his burden will fall from your shoulders,
and his yoke from your neck.
The yoke will be broken because your neck will be too large.
²⁸ Assyria has come to Aiath
and has gone through Migron,
storing their equipment at Michmash.
²⁹ They crossed over at the ford, saying,
"We will spend the night at Geba."
The people of Ramah are trembling;
those at Gibeah of Saul have fled.
³⁰ Cry aloud, daughter of Gallim!
Listen, Laishah!
Anathoth is miserable.
³¹ Madmenah has fled.
The inhabitants of Gebim have sought refuge.
³² Today the Assyrians will stand at Nob,
shaking their fists at the mountain of Daughter Zion,
the hill of Jerusalem.
³³ Look, the Lord GOD of Armies
will chop off the branches with terrifying power,
and the tall trees will be cut down,
the high trees felled.
³⁴ He is clearing the thickets of the forest with an ax,
and Lebanon with its majesty will fall.

ISAIAH 11

REIGN OF THE DAVIDIC KING

¹ Then a shoot will grow from the stump of Jesse,
and a branch from his roots will bear fruit.
² The Spirit of the LORD will rest on him—
a Spirit of wisdom and understanding,
a Spirit of counsel and strength,
a Spirit of knowledge and of the fear of the LORD.
³ His delight will be in the fear of the LORD.

NOTES

He will not judge
by what he sees with his eyes,
he will not execute justice
by what he hears with his ears,
⁴ but he will judge the poor righteously
and execute justice for the oppressed of
   the land.
He will strike the land
with a scepter from his mouth,
and he will kill the wicked
with a command from his lips.
⁵ Righteousness will be a belt around his hips;
faithfulness will be a belt around his waist.

⁶ The wolf will dwell with the lamb,
and the leopard will lie down with the goat.
The calf, the young lion, and the fattened calf
   will be together,
and a child will lead them.
⁷ The cow and the bear will graze,
their young ones will lie down together,
and the lion will eat straw like cattle.
⁸ An infant will play beside the cobra's pit,
and a toddler will put his hand into a
   snake's den.
⁹ They will not harm or destroy each other
on my entire holy mountain,
for the land will be as full
of the knowledge of the Lord
as the sea is filled with water.

ISRAEL REGATHERED

¹⁰ On that day the root of Jesse
will stand as a banner for the peoples.
The nations will look to him for guidance,
and his resting place will be glorious.

¹¹ On that day the Lord will extend his hand a second time to recover the remnant of his people who survive—from Assyria, Egypt, Pathros, Cush, Elam, Shinar, Hamath, and the coasts and islands of the west.

¹² He will lift up a banner for the nations
and gather the dispersed of Israel;
he will collect the scattered of Judah
from the four corners of the earth.
¹³ Ephraim's envy will cease;
Judah's harassing will end.
Ephraim will no longer be envious of Judah,
and Judah will not harass Ephraim.
¹⁴ But they will swoop down
on the Philistine flank to the west.
Together they will plunder the people of
   the east.
They will extend their power over Edom
   and Moab,
and the Ammonites will be their subjects.
¹⁵ The Lord will divide the Gulf of Suez.
He will wave his hand over the Euphrates
with his mighty wind
and will split it into seven streams,
letting people walk through on foot.
¹⁶ There will be a highway for the remnant
   of his people
who will survive from Assyria,
as there was for Israel
when they came up from the land of Egypt.

ISAIAH 12

A SONG OF PRAISE

¹ On that day you will say:
"I will give thanks to you, Lord,
although you were angry with me.
Your anger has turned away,
and you have comforted me.
² Indeed, God is my salvation;
I will trust him and not be afraid,
for the Lord, the Lord himself,

is my strength and my song.
He has become my salvation."
³ You will joyfully draw water
from the springs of salvation,
⁴ and on that day you will say,
"Give thanks to the LORD; proclaim his name!
Make his works known among the peoples.
Declare that his name is exalted.
⁵ Sing to the LORD, for he has done glorious things.
Let this be known throughout the earth.
⁶ Cry out and sing, citizen of Zion,
for the Holy One of Israel is among you
in his greatness."

GOING DEEPER

COLOSSIANS 1:13

He has rescued us from the domain of darkness and transferred us into the kingdom of the Son he loves.

WEEK ONE
RESPONSE

USE THE FOLLOWING WORKSHEET TO HELP YOU REFLECT ON THIS WEEK'S READING.

Places or people the prophecies in this week's reading were directed toward:

An encouraging or challenging verse:

Isaiah :

A question to ponder and investigate:

Descriptive details about God and His people:

God

His People

How God's people were called to respond:

Specific sins revealed or warnings given:

GOD'S HOLINESS

How was God's holiness demonstrated in this week's reading?
Consider the ways God was described (turn to page 164 for suggestions) or God's own words or actions to help shape your answer.

Circle one expression of His holiness in your answer above that stands out to you. How might trusting in this aspect of God strengthen your faith this Lenten season?

THE PEOPLE'S SIN

Review the sins that you listed on the previous page and consider how some of them may be present in your own life, even if they are expressed in different ways. Circle one that stands out to you and then use this space to reflect on the ways this sin appears in your own life.
Consider what often leads you to commit this sin and how it impacts you and the people around you.

HOPE FOR SALVATION THROUGH GOD

God responds to His people's sin and rebellion with a promise to save and restore them. Looking back on this week's reading, highlight or underline some of God's promises to His people.

Having reflected on God's holiness and the reality of sin, how do these messages of hope encourage you as you journey through this season of Lent?
Consider how Jesus has fulfilled these promises (turn to page 214 for suggestions) and how that can give you specific, tangible hope today.

DAY 6

GRACE DAY

SECTION 1

Take this day to catch up on your reading, pray, and rest in the presence of the Lord.

NOW MAY THE GOD OF PEACE HIMSELF SANCTIFY YOU COMPLETELY. AND MAY YOUR WHOLE SPIRIT, SOUL, AND BODY BE KEPT SOUND AND BLAMELESS AT THE COMING OF OUR LORD JESUS CHRIST. HE WHO CALLS YOU IS FAITHFUL; HE WILL DO IT.

1 THESSALONIANS 5:23–24

WEEKLY   DAY ―――――――

Scripture is God breathed and true. When we memorize it, we carry His Word with us wherever we go.

During this reading plan, we will memorize our key verse, Isaiah 43:1. We'll memorize a portion of the verse each week and spend time committing the whole verse to memory at the end of Week 5. This week, we'll start with the first line of the verse.

SEE TIPS FOR MEMORIZING SCRIPTURE ON PAGE 272.

7 — TRUTH

ISAIAH 43:1

<u>Now this is what the Lord says</u>—the one who created you, Jacob, and the one who formed you, Israel—"Do not fear, for I have redeemed you; I have called you by your name; you are mine."

A PRONOUNCEMENT AGAINST BABYLON

DAY 8 — **SECTION 1**

ISAIAH 13

A PRONOUNCEMENT AGAINST BABYLON

¹ A pronouncement concerning Babylon that Isaiah son of Amoz saw:

² Lift up a banner on a barren mountain.
Call out to them.
Signal with your hand, and they will go
through the gates of the nobles.
³ I have commanded my consecrated ones;
yes, I have called my warriors,
who celebrate my triumph,
to execute my wrath.
⁴ Listen, a commotion on the mountains,
like that of a mighty people!
Listen, an uproar among the kingdoms,
like nations being gathered together!
The LORD of Armies is mobilizing an army
   for war.
⁵ They are coming from a distant land,
from the farthest horizon—
the LORD and the weapons of his wrath—
to destroy the whole country.
⁶ Wail! For the day of the LORD is near.
It will come as destruction from
   the Almighty.
⁷ Therefore everyone's hands will
   become weak,
and every man will lose heart.
⁸ They will be horrified;
pain and agony will seize them;
they will be in anguish like a woman
   in labor.
They will look at each other,
their faces flushed with fear.
⁹ Look, the day of the LORD is coming—
cruel, with fury and burning anger—
to make the earth a desolation

and to destroy its sinners.
¹⁰ Indeed, the stars of the sky and
    its constellations
will not give their light.
The sun will be dark when it rises,
and the moon will not shine.
¹¹ I will punish the world for its evil,
and wicked people for their iniquities.
I will put an end to the pride of the arrogant
and humiliate the insolence of tyrants.
¹² I will make a human more scarce than
    fine gold,
and mankind more rare than the gold
    of Ophir.
¹³ Therefore I will make the heavens tremble,
and the earth will shake from its foundations
at the wrath of the Lord of Armies,
on the day of his burning anger.
¹⁴ Like wandering gazelles
and like sheep without a shepherd,
each one will turn to his own people,
each one will flee to his own land.
¹⁵ Whoever is found will be stabbed,
and whoever is caught will die by the sword.
¹⁶ Their children will be dashed to pieces
    before their eyes;
their houses will be looted,
and their wives raped.
¹⁷ Look! I am stirring up the Medes
    against them,
who cannot be bought off with silver
and who have no desire for gold.
¹⁸ Their bows will cut young men to pieces.
They will have no compassion on offspring;
they will not look with pity on children.

¹⁹ And Babylon, the jewel of the kingdoms,
the glory of the pride of the Chaldeans,
will be like Sodom and Gomorrah
when God overthrew them.
²⁰ It will never be inhabited
or lived in from generation to generation;
a nomad will not pitch his tent there,
and shepherds will not let their flocks
    rest there.
²¹ But desert creatures will lie down there,
and owls will fill the houses.
Ostriches will dwell there,
and wild goats will leap about.
²² Hyenas will howl in the fortresses,
and jackals, in the luxurious palaces.
Babylon's time is almost up;
her days are almost over.

ISAIAH 14

ISRAEL'S RETURN

¹ For the Lord will have compassion on Jacob and will choose Israel again. He will settle them on their own land. The resident alien will join them and be united with the house of Jacob. ² The nations will escort Israel and bring it to its homeland. Then the house of Israel will possess them as male and female slaves in the Lord's land. They will make captives of their captors and will rule over their oppressors.

DOWNFALL OF THE KING OF BABYLON

³ When the Lord gives you rest from your pain, torment, and the hard labor you were forced to do, ⁴ you will sing this song of contempt about the king of Babylon and say:

How the oppressor has quieted down,
and how the raging has become quiet!
⁵ The Lord has broken the staff of
    the wicked,
the scepter of the rulers.
⁶ It struck the peoples in anger
with unceasing blows.
It subdued the nations in rage
with relentless persecution.
⁷ The whole earth is calm and at rest;

people shout with a ringing cry.
⁸ Even the cypresses and the cedars of Lebanon
rejoice over you:
"Since you have been laid low,
no lumberjack has come against us."

⁹ Sheol below is eager to greet your coming,
stirring up the spirits of the departed for you—
all the rulers of the earth—
making all the kings of the nations
rise from their thrones.
¹⁰ They all respond to you, saying,
"You too have become as weak as we are;
you have become like us!
¹¹ Your splendor has been brought down to Sheol,
along with the music of your harps.
Maggots are spread out under you,
and worms cover you."

¹² Shining morning star,
how you have fallen from the heavens!
You destroyer of nations,
you have been cut down to the ground.
¹³ You said to yourself,
"I will ascend to the heavens;
I will set up my throne
above the stars of God.
I will sit on the mount of the gods' assembly,
in the remotest parts of the North.
¹⁴ I will ascend above the highest clouds;
I will make myself like the Most High."
¹⁵ But you will be brought down to Sheol
into the deepest regions of the Pit.

¹⁶ Those who see you will stare at you;
they will look closely at you:
"Is this the man who caused the earth to tremble,
who shook the kingdoms,
¹⁷ who turned the world into a wilderness,
who destroyed its cities
and would not release the prisoners to return home?"
¹⁸ All the kings of the nations

lie in splendor, each in his own tomb.
¹⁹ But you are thrown out without a grave,
like a worthless branch,
covered by those slain with the sword
and dumped into a rocky pit like a
    trampled corpse.
²⁰ You will not join them in burial,
because you destroyed your land
and slaughtered your own people.
The offspring of evildoers
will never be mentioned again.
²¹ Prepare a place of slaughter for his sons,
because of the iniquity of their ancestors.
They will never rise up to possess a land
or fill the surface of the earth with cities.

²² "I will rise up against them"—this is the declaration of the Lord of Armies—"and I will cut off from Babylon her reputation, remnant, offspring, and posterity"—this is the Lord's declaration. ²³ "I will make her a swampland and a region for herons, and I will sweep her away with the broom of destruction."

> This is the declaration of the Lord
>   of Armies.

ASSYRIA WILL BE DESTROYED

²⁴ The Lord of Armies has sworn:

> As I have purposed, so it will be;
> as I have planned it, so it will happen.
> ²⁵ I will break Assyria in my land;
> I will tread him down on my mountain.
> Then his yoke will be taken from them,
> and his burden will be removed from
>   their shoulders.
> ²⁶ This is the plan prepared
> for the whole earth,
> and this is the hand stretched out
> against all the nations.

²⁷ The Lord of Armies himself has
    planned it;
therefore, who can stand in its way?
It is his hand that is outstretched,
so who can turn it back?

A PRONOUNCEMENT AGAINST PHILISTIA

²⁸ In the year that King Ahaz died, this pronouncement came:

> ²⁹ Don't rejoice, all of you in Philistia,
> because the rod of the one who struck
>   you is broken.
> For a viper will come from the root of
>   a snake,
> and from its egg comes a flying serpent.
> ³⁰ Then the firstborn of the poor will be
>   well fed,
> and the impoverished will lie down in safety,
> but I will kill your root with hunger,
> and your remnant will be slain.
> ³¹ Wail, you gates! Cry out, city!
> Tremble with fear, all Philistia!
> For a cloud of dust is coming from the north,
> and there is no one missing from the
>   invader's ranks.
> ³² What answer will be given to the
>   messengers from that nation?
> The Lord has founded Zion,
> and his oppressed people find refuge in her.

🕮 GOING DEEPER

ROMANS 11:30-36

³⁰ As you once disobeyed God but now have received mercy through their disobedience, ³¹ so they too have now disobeyed, resulting in mercy to you, so that they also may now receive mercy.

⁣³² For God has imprisoned all in disobedience so that he may have mercy on all.

A HYMN OF PRAISE

    ³³ Oh, the depth of the riches
    and the wisdom and the knowledge of God!
    How unsearchable his judgments
    and untraceable his ways!
    ³⁴ For who has known the mind of the Lord?
    Or who has been his counselor?
    ³⁵ And who has ever given to God,
    that he should be repaid?
    ³⁶ For from him and through him
    and to him are all things.
    To him be the glory forever. Amen.

NOTES

A PRONOUNCEMENT CONCERNING MOAB

WHEN THE OPPRESSOR HAS GONE, DESTRUCTION HAS ENDED, AND MARAUDERS HAVE VANISHED FROM THE LAND, A THRONE WILL BE ESTABLISHED IN LOVE, AND ONE WILL SIT ON IT FAITHFULLY IN THE TENT OF DAVID, JUDGING AND PURSUING WHAT IS RIGHT, QUICK TO EXECUTE JUSTICE.

ISAIAH 16:4–5

DAY 9 — SECTION 1

ISAIAH 15

A PRONOUNCEMENT AGAINST MOAB

¹ A pronouncement concerning Moab:

Ar in Moab is devastated,
destroyed in a night.
Kir in Moab is devastated,
destroyed in a night.
² Dibon went up to its temple
to weep at its high places.
Moab wails on Nebo and at Medeba.
Every head is shaved;
every beard is chopped short.

³ In its streets they wear sackcloth;
on its rooftops and in its public squares everyone wails,
falling down and weeping.
⁴ Heshbon and Elealeh cry out;
their voices are heard as far away as Jahaz.
Therefore the soldiers of Moab cry out,
and they tremble.
⁵ My heart cries out over Moab,
whose fugitives flee as far as Zoar,
to Eglath-shelishiyah;
they go up the Ascent of Luhith weeping;
they raise a cry of destruction
on the road to Horonaim.

⁶ The Waters of Nimrim are desolate;
the grass is withered, the foliage is gone,
and the vegetation has vanished.
⁷ So they carry their wealth and belongings
over the Wadi of the Willows.
⁸ For their cry echoes
throughout the territory of Moab.
Their wailing reaches Eglaim;
their wailing reaches Beer-elim.
⁹ The Waters of Dibon are full of blood,
but I will bring on Dibon even more than this—
a lion for those who escape from Moab,
and for the survivors in the land.

ISAIAH 16

¹ Send lambs to the ruler of the land,
from Sela in the desert
to the mountain of Daughter Zion.
² Like a bird fleeing,
forced from the nest,
the daughters of Moab
will be at the fords of the Arnon.
³ Give us counsel and make a decision.
Shelter us at noonday
with shade that is as dark as night.
Hide the refugees;
do not betray the one who flees.
⁴ Let my refugees stay with you;
be a refuge for Moab from the aggressor.
When the oppressor has gone,
destruction has ended,
and marauders have vanished from the land,

⁵ a throne will be established in love,
and one will sit on it faithfully
in the tent of David,
judging and pursuing what is right,
quick to execute justice.
⁶ We have heard of Moab's pride—
how very proud he is—
his haughtiness, his pride, his arrogance,
and his empty boasting.
⁷ Therefore let Moab wail;
let every one of them wail for Moab.
You who are completely devastated, mourn
for the raisin cakes of Kir-hareseth.
⁸ For Heshbon's terraced vineyards
and the grapevines of Sibmah have withered.
The rulers of the nations
have trampled its choice vines
that reached as far as Jazer
and spread to the desert.
Their shoots spread out
and reached the sea.
⁹ So I join with Jazer
to weep for the vines of Sibmah;
I drench Heshbon and Elealeh with my tears.
Triumphant shouts have fallen silent
over your summer fruit and your harvest.
¹⁰ Joy and rejoicing have been removed from
the orchard;
no one is singing or shouting for joy in
the vineyards.
No one tramples grapes in the winepresses.
I have put an end to the shouting.

¹¹ Therefore I moan like the sound of a lyre
for Moab,
as does my innermost being for Kir-heres.
¹² When Moab appears
and tires himself out on the high place
and comes to his sanctuary to pray,
it will do him no good.

¹³ This is the message that the LORD previously announced about Moab. ¹⁴ And now the LORD says, "In three years, as a hired worker counts years, Moab's splendor will become an object of contempt, in spite of a very large population. And those who are left will be few and weak."

💜 GOING DEEPER

PSALM 13:3-6

³ Consider me and answer, LORD my God.
Restore brightness to my eyes;
otherwise, I will sleep in death.
⁴ My enemy will say, "I have triumphed
over him,"
and my foes will rejoice because I am shaken.

⁵ But I have trusted in your faithful love;
my heart will rejoice in your deliverance.

⁶ I will sing to the LORD
because he has treated me generously.

NOTES

HEBREWS 1:1-3, 8-9

THE NATURE OF THE SON

¹ Long ago God spoke to our ancestors by the prophets at different times and in different ways. ² In these last days, he has spoken to us by his Son. God has appointed him heir of all things and made the universe through him. ³ The Son is the radiance of God's glory and the exact expression of his nature, sustaining all things by his powerful word. After making purification for sins, he sat down at the right hand of the Majesty on high.

…

⁸ but to the Son:

> Your throne, God,
> is forever and ever,
> and the scepter of your kingdom
> is a scepter of justice.
> ⁹ You have loved righteousness
> and hated lawlessness;
> this is why God, your God,
> has anointed you
> with the oil of joy
> beyond your companions.

DAY 10 SECTION 1

JUDGMENT AGAINST ISRAEL

ISAIAH 17

A PRONOUNCEMENT AGAINST DAMASCUS

¹ A pronouncement concerning Damascus:

> Look, Damascus is no longer a city.
> It has become a ruined heap.
> ² The cities of Aroer are abandoned;
> they will be places for flocks.
> They will lie down without fear.
>
> ³ The fortress disappears from Ephraim,
> and a kingdom from Damascus.
> The remnant of Aram will be
> like the splendor of the Israelites.
>
>   This is the declaration of the Lord of Armies.

JUDGMENT AGAINST ISRAEL

> ⁴ On that day
> the splendor of Jacob will fade,
> and his healthy body will become emaciated.
> ⁵ It will be as if a reaper had gathered standing grain—
> his arm harvesting the heads of grain—

and as if one had gleaned heads of grain
in Rephaim Valley.

⁶ Only gleanings will be left in Israel,
as if an olive tree had been beaten—
two or three olives at the very top of the tree,
four or five on its fruitful branches.
This is the declaration of the Lord, the God of Israel.

⁷ On that day people will look to their Maker and will turn their eyes to the Holy One of Israel.

⁸ They will not look to the altars they made with their hands or to the Asherahs and shrines they made with their fingers.

⁹ On that day their strong cities will be
like the abandoned woods and mountaintops
that were abandoned because of the Israelites;
there will be desolation.

¹⁰ For you have forgotten the God of your salvation,
and you have failed to remember
the rock of your strength;
therefore you will plant beautiful plants
and set out cuttings from exotic vines.
¹¹ On the day that you plant,
you will help them to grow,
and in the morning
you will help your seed to sprout,
but the harvest will vanish
on the day of disease and incurable pain.

JUDGMENT AGAINST THE NATIONS

¹² Ah! The roar of many peoples—
they roar like the roaring of the seas.
The raging of the nations—
they rage like the rumble of rushing water.
¹³ The nations rage like the rumble of a huge torrent.
He rebukes them, and they flee far away,
driven before the wind like chaff on the hills

and like tumbleweeds before a gale.
¹⁴ In the evening—sudden terror!
Before morning—it is gone!
This is the fate of those who plunder us
and the lot of those who ravage us.

ISAIAH 18

THE LORD'S MESSAGE TO CUSH

¹ Woe to the land of buzzing insect wings
beyond the rivers of Cush,
² which sends envoys by sea,
in reed vessels over the water.
Go, swift messengers,
to a nation tall and smooth-skinned,
to a people feared far and near,
a powerful nation with a strange language,
whose land is divided by rivers.
³ All you inhabitants of the world
and you who live on the earth,
when a banner is raised on the mountains, look!
When a ram's horn sounds, listen!

⁴ For the LORD said to me:

I will quietly look out from my place,
like shimmering heat in sunshine,
like a rain cloud in harvest heat.
⁵ For before the harvest, when the blossoming is over
and the blossom becomes a ripening grape,
he will cut off the shoots with a pruning knife,
and tear away and remove the branches.
⁶ They will all be left for the birds of prey on the hills
and for the wild animals of the land.
The birds of prey will spend the summer feeding on them,
and all the wild animals the winter.

⁷ At that time a gift will be brought to the LORD of Armies from a people tall and smooth-skinned, a people feared far and near, a powerful nation with a strange language, whose land is divided by rivers—to Mount Zion, the place of the name of the LORD of Armies.

♥ GOING DEEPER

LEVITICUS 26:1-2, 14-17

COVENANT BLESSINGS AND DISCIPLINE

¹ "Do not make worthless idols for yourselves, set up a carved image or sacred pillar for yourselves, or place a sculpted stone in your land to bow down to it, for I am the LORD your God. ² Keep my Sabbaths and revere my sanctuary; I am the LORD."

…

¹⁴ "But if you do not obey me and observe all these commands— ¹⁵ if you reject my statutes and despise my ordinances, and do not observe all my commands—and break my covenant, ¹⁶ then I will do this to you: I will bring terror on you—wasting disease and fever that will cause your eyes to fail and your life to ebb away. You will sow your seed in vain because your enemies will eat it. ¹⁷ I will turn against you, so that you will be defeated by your enemies. Those who hate you will rule over you, and you will flee even though no one is pursuing you."

1 CORINTHIANS 10:14-22

WARNING AGAINST IDOLATRY

¹⁴ So then, my dear friends, flee from idolatry. ¹⁵ I am speaking as to sensible people. Judge for yourselves what I am saying. ¹⁶ The cup of blessing that we bless, is it not a sharing in the

blood of Christ? The bread that we break, is it not a sharing in the body of Christ? [17] Because there is one bread, we who are many are one body, since all of us share the one bread. [18] Consider the people of Israel. Do not those who eat the sacrifices participate in the altar? [19] What am I saying then? That food sacrificed to idols is anything, or that an idol is anything? [20] No, but I do say that what they sacrifice, they sacrifice to demons and not to God. I do not want you to be participants with demons! [21] You cannot drink the cup of the Lord and the cup of demons. You cannot share in the Lord's table and the table of demons. [22] Or are we provoking the Lord to jealousy? Are we stronger than he?

NOTES

DAY 11

A PRONOUNCEMENT AGAINST EGYPT

SECTION 1

ISAIAH 19

A PRONOUNCEMENT AGAINST EGYPT

¹ A pronouncement concerning Egypt:

Look, the Lord rides on a swift cloud
and is coming to Egypt.
Egypt's worthless idols will tremble before him,
and Egypt will lose heart.
² I will provoke Egyptians against Egyptians;
each will fight against his brother
and each against his friend,
city against city, kingdom against kingdom.
³ Egypt's spirit will be disturbed within it,
and I will frustrate its plans.
Then they will inquire of worthless idols, ghosts,
mediums, and spiritists.

⁴ I will hand over Egypt to harsh masters,
and a strong king will rule it.
    This is the declaration of the Lord God of Armies.
⁵ The water of the sea will dry up,
and the river will be parched and dry.
⁶ The channels will stink;
they will dwindle, and Egypt's canals will be parched.
Reed and rush will wilt.
⁷ The reeds by the Nile, by the mouth of the river,
and all the cultivated areas of the Nile
will wither, blow away, and vanish.
⁸ Then the fishermen will mourn.
All those who cast hooks into the Nile will lament,
and those who spread nets on the water will give up.
⁹ Those who work with flax will be dismayed;
those combing it and weaving linen will turn pale.
¹⁰ Egypt's weavers will be dejected;
all her wage earners will be demoralized.
¹¹ The princes of Zoan are complete fools;
Pharaoh's wisest advisers give stupid advice!
How can you say to Pharaoh,
"I am one of the wise,
a student of eastern kings"?
¹² Where then are your wise men?

Let them tell you and reveal
what the Lord of Armies has planned against Egypt.
¹³ The princes of Zoan have been fools;
the princes of Memphis are deceived.
Her tribal chieftains have led Egypt astray.

¹⁴ The Lord has mixed within her a spirit of confusion.
The leaders have made Egypt stagger in all she does,
as a drunkard staggers in his vomit.
¹⁵ No head or tail, palm or reed,
will be able to do anything for Egypt.

EGYPT WILL KNOW THE LORD

¹⁶ On that day Egypt will be like women and will tremble with fear because of the threatening hand of the Lord of Armies when he raises it against them. ¹⁷ The land of Judah will terrify Egypt; whenever Judah is mentioned, Egypt will tremble because of what the Lord of Armies has planned against it.

¹⁸ On that day five cities in the land of Egypt will speak the language of Canaan and swear loyalty to the Lord of Armies. One of the cities will be called the City of the Sun.

¹⁹ On that day there will be an altar to the Lord in the center of the land of Egypt and a pillar to the Lord near her border. ²⁰ It will be a sign and witness to the Lord of Armies in the land of Egypt. When they cry out to the Lord because of their oppressors, he will send them a savior and leader, and he will rescue them. ²¹ The Lord will make himself known to Egypt, and Egypt will know the Lord on that day. They will offer sacrifices and offerings; they will make vows to the Lord and fulfill them. ²² The Lord will strike Egypt, striking and healing. Then they will turn to the Lord, and he will be receptive to their prayers and heal them.

²³ On that day there will be a highway from Egypt to Assyria. Assyria will go to Egypt, Egypt to Assyria, and Egypt will worship with Assyria.

²⁴ On that day Israel will form a triple alliance with Egypt and Assyria—a blessing within the land. ²⁵ The Lord of Armies will bless them, saying, "Egypt my people, Assyria my handiwork, and Israel my inheritance are blessed."

ISAIAH 20

NO HELP FROM CUSH OR EGYPT

¹ In the year that the chief commander, sent by King Sargon of Assyria, came to Ashdod and attacked and captured it— ² during that time the LORD had spoken through Isaiah son of Amoz, saying, "Go, take off your sackcloth from your waist and remove the sandals from your feet," and he did that, going stripped and barefoot— ³ the LORD said, "As my servant Isaiah has gone stripped and barefoot three years as a sign and omen against Egypt and Cush, ⁴ so the king of Assyria will lead the captives of Egypt and the exiles of Cush, young and old alike, stripped and barefoot, with bared buttocks—to Egypt's shame. ⁵ Those who made Cush their hope and Egypt their boast will be dismayed and ashamed. ⁶ And the inhabitants of this coastland will say on that day, 'Look, this is what has happened to those we relied on and fled to for help to rescue us from the king of Assyria! Now, how will we escape?'"

ISAIAH 21

A JUDGMENT ON BABYLON

¹ A pronouncement concerning the desert by the sea:

> Like storms that pass over the Negev,
> it comes from the desert, from the land of terror.
> ² A troubling vision is declared to me:
> "The treacherous one acts treacherously,
> and the destroyer destroys.
> Advance, Elam! Lay siege, you Medes!
> I will put an end to all the groaning."
> ³ Therefore I am filled with anguish.
> Pain grips me, like the pain of a woman in labor.
> I am too perplexed to hear,
> too dismayed to see.
> ⁴ My heart staggers;
> horror terrifies me.
> He has turned my last glimmer of hope
> into sheer terror.
> ⁵ Prepare a table, and spread out a carpet!
> Eat and drink!
> Rise up, you princes, and oil the shields!

NOTES

⁶ For the Lord has said to me,
"Go, post a lookout;
let him report what he sees.
⁷ When he sees riders—
pairs of horsemen,
riders on donkeys,
riders on camels—
he must pay close attention."
⁸ Then the lookout reported,
"Lord, I stand on the watchtower all day,
and I stay at my post all night.
⁹ Look, riders come—
horsemen in pairs."
And he answered, saying,
"Babylon has fallen, has fallen.
All the images of her gods
have been shattered on the ground."
¹⁰ My people who have been crushed
on the threshing floor,
I have declared to you
what I have heard from the Lord of Armies,
the God of Israel.

A PRONOUNCEMENT AGAINST DUMAH

¹¹ A pronouncement concerning Dumah:

One calls to me from Seir,
"Watchman, what is left of the night?
Watchman, what is left of the night?"
¹² The watchman said,
"Morning has come, and also night.
If you want to ask, ask!
Come back again."

A PRONOUNCEMENT AGAINST ARABIA

¹³ A pronouncement concerning Arabia:

In the desert brush
you will camp for the night,
you caravans of Dedanites.

¹⁴ Bring water for the thirsty.
The inhabitants of the land of Tema
meet the refugees with food.
¹⁵ For they have fled from swords,
from the drawn sword,
from the bow that is strung,
and from the stress of battle.

¹⁶ For the Lord said this to me: "Within one year, as a hired worker counts years, all the glory of Kedar will be gone. ¹⁷ The remaining Kedarite archers will be few in number." For the LORD, the God of Israel, has spoken.

GOING DEEPER

ROMANS 9:14–18

GOD'S SELECTION IS JUST

¹⁴ What should we say then? Is there injustice with God? Absolutely not! ¹⁵ For he tells Moses, I will show mercy to whom I will show mercy, and I will have compassion on whom I will have compassion.

> ¹⁶ So then, it does not depend on human will or effort but on God who shows mercy.

¹⁷ For the Scripture tells Pharaoh, I raised you up for this reason so that I may display my power in you and that my name may be proclaimed in the whole earth. ¹⁸ So then, he has mercy on whom he wants to have mercy and he hardens whom he wants to harden.

A PRONOUNCEMENT AGAINST JERUSALEM

DAY 12   SECTION 1

ISAIAH 22

A PRONOUNCEMENT AGAINST JERUSALEM

¹ A pronouncement concerning the Valley of Vision:

What's the matter with you?
Why have all of you gone up to the rooftops?
² The noisy city, the jubilant town,
is filled with celebration.
Your dead did not die by the sword;
they were not killed in battle.
³ All your rulers have fled together,
captured without a bow.
All your fugitives were captured together;
they had fled far away.
⁴ Therefore I said,
"Look away from me! Let me weep bitterly!
Do not try to comfort me
about the destruction of my dear people."
⁵ For the Lord GOD of Armies
had a day of tumult, trampling,
    and confusion
in the Valley of Vision—
people shouting and crying to the mountains;
⁶ Elam took up a quiver
with chariots and horsemen,
and Kir uncovered the shield.
⁷ Your best valleys were full of chariots,
and horsemen were positioned at the
    city gates.
⁸ He removed the defenses of Judah.

On that day you looked to the weapons in the House of the Forest. ⁹ You saw that there were many breaches in the walls of the city of David. You collected water from the lower pool. ¹⁰ You counted the houses of Jerusalem so that you could tear them down to fortify the wall. ¹¹ You made a reservoir between the walls for the water of the ancient pool, but you did not look to the one who made it, or consider the one who created it long ago.

¹² On that day the Lord GOD of Armies
called for weeping, for wailing, for
    shaven heads,
and for the wearing of sackcloth.
¹³ But look: joy and gladness,
butchering of cattle, slaughtering of sheep
    and goats,
eating of meat, and drinking of wine—
"Let's eat and drink, for tomorrow we die!"
¹⁴ The LORD of Armies has directly revealed
    to me:

"This iniquity will not be wiped out for you people as long as you live." The Lord God of Armies has spoken.

A PRONOUNCEMENT AGAINST SHEBNA

¹⁵ The Lord God of Armies said, "Go to Shebna, that steward who is in charge of the palace, and say to him: ¹⁶ What are you doing here? Who authorized you to carve out a tomb for yourself here, carving your tomb on the height and cutting a resting place for yourself out of rock? ¹⁷ Look, you strong man! The Lord is about to shake you violently. He will take hold of you, ¹⁸ wind you up into a ball, and sling you into a wide land. There you will die, and there your glorious chariots will be—a disgrace to the house of your lord. ¹⁹ I will remove you from your office; you will be ousted from your position.

²⁰ "On that day I will call for my servant, Eliakim son of Hilkiah. ²¹ I will clothe him with your robe and tie your sash around him. I will hand your authority over to him, and he will be like a father to the inhabitants of Jerusalem and to the house of Judah. ²² I will place the key of the house of David on his shoulder; what he opens, no one can close; what he closes, no one can open. ²³ I will drive him, like a peg, into a firm place. He will be a throne of honor for his father's family. ²⁴ They will hang on him all the glory of his father's family: the descendants and the offshoots—all the small vessels, from bowls to every kind of jar. ²⁵ On that day"—the declaration of the Lord of Armies—"the peg that was driven into a firm place will give way, be cut off, and fall, and the load on it will be destroyed." Indeed, the Lord has spoken.

ISAIAH 23

A PRONOUNCEMENT AGAINST TYRE

¹ A pronouncement concerning Tyre:

> Wail, ships of Tarshish,
> for your haven has been destroyed.
> Word has reached them from the land of Cyprus.
> ² Mourn, inhabitants of the coastland,
> you merchants of Sidon;
> your agents have crossed the sea
> ³ over deep water.
> Tyre's revenue was the grain from Shihor—

NOTES

the harvest of the Nile.
She was the merchant among the nations.
⁴ Be ashamed, Sidon, the stronghold of
   the sea,
for the sea has spoken:
"I have not been in labor or given birth.
I have not raised young men
or brought up young women."
⁵ When the news reaches Egypt,
they will be in anguish over the news
   about Tyre.
⁶ Cross over to Tarshish;
wail, inhabitants of the coastland!
⁷ Is this your jubilant city,
whose origin was in ancient times,
whose feet have taken her
to reside far away?
⁸ Who planned this against Tyre,
the bestower of crowns,
whose traders are princes,
whose merchants are the honored ones of
   the earth?
⁹ The LORD of Armies planned it,
to desecrate all its glorious beauty,
to disgrace all the honored ones of the earth.
¹⁰ Overflow your land like the Nile, daughter
   of Tarshish;
there is no longer anything to restrain you.
¹¹ He stretched out his hand over the sea;
he made kingdoms tremble.
The LORD has commanded
that the Canaanite fortresses be destroyed.
¹² He said,
"You will not celebrate anymore,
ravished young woman, daughter of Sidon.
Get up and cross over to Cyprus—
even there you will have no rest!"
¹³ Look at the land of the Chaldeans—
a people who no longer exist.
Assyria destined it for desert creatures.
They set up their siege towers
and stripped its palaces.
They made it a ruin.
¹⁴ Wail, ships of Tarshish,
because your fortress is destroyed!

¹⁵ On that day Tyre will be forgotten for seventy years—the life span of one king. At the end of seventy years, what the song says about the prostitute will happen to Tyre:

¹⁶ Pick up your lyre,
stroll through the city,
you forgotten prostitute.
Play skillfully,
sing many a song
so that you will be remembered.

¹⁷ And at the end of the seventy years, the LORD will restore Tyre and she will go back into business, prostituting herself with all the kingdoms of the world throughout the earth. ¹⁸ But her profits and wages will be dedicated to the LORD. They will not be stored or saved, for her profit will go to those who live in the LORD's presence, to provide them with ample food and sacred clothing.

GOING DEEPER

PSALM 74:1-2, 20-23

PRAYER FOR ISRAEL

A Maskil of Asaph.

¹ Why have you rejected us forever, God?
Why does your anger burn
against the sheep of your pasture?
² Remember your congregation,
which you purchased long ago

and redeemed as the tribe for your own possession.
Remember Mount Zion where you dwell.

…

[20] Consider the covenant,
for the dark places of the land are full of violence.
[21] Do not let the oppressed turn away in shame;
let the poor and needy praise your name.
[22] Rise up, God, champion your cause!
Remember the insults
that fools bring against you all day long.
[23] Do not forget the clamor of your adversaries,
the tumult of your opponents that goes up constantly.

1 CORINTHIANS 15:31–34

[31] I face death every day, as surely as I may boast about you, brothers and sisters, in Christ Jesus our Lord. [32] If I fought wild beasts in Ephesus as a mere man, what good did that do me? If the dead are not raised, Let us eat and drink, for tomorrow we die. [33] Do not be deceived: "Bad company corrupts good morals."

[34] Come to your senses and stop sinning; for some people are ignorant about God.

I say this to your shame.

NOTES

WEEK TWO
RESPONSE

USE THE FOLLOWING WORKSHEET TO HELP YOU REFLECT ON THIS WEEK'S READING.

Places or people the prophecies in this week's reading were directed toward:

An encouraging or challenging verse:

Isaiah

A question to ponder and investigate:

Descriptive details about God and His people:

God

His People

Specific sins revealed or warnings given:

How God's people were called to respond:

GOD'S HOLINESS

How was God's holiness demonstrated in this week's reading?

Circle one expression of His holiness in your answer above that stands out to you. How might trusting in this aspect of God strengthen your faith this Lenten season?

THE PEOPLE'S SIN

Review the sins that you listed on the previous page and consider how some of them may be present in your own life, even if they are expressed in different ways. Circle one that stands out to you and then use this space to reflect on the ways this sin appears in your own life.

HOPE FOR SALVATION THROUGH GOD

God responds to His people's sin and rebellion with a promise to save and restore them. Looking back on this week's reading, highlight or underline some of God's promises to His people.

Having reflected on God's holiness and the reality of sin, how do these messages of hope encourage you as you journey through this season of Lent?

DAY 13

GRACE DAY

SECTION 1

Take this day to catch up on your reading, pray, and rest in the presence of the Lord.

BUT I HAVE TRUSTED IN YOUR FAITHFUL LOVE; MY HEART WILL REJOICE IN YOUR DELIVERANCE.

PSALM 13:5

WEEKLY

DAY _____

Scripture is God breathed and true. When we memorize it, we carry His Word with us wherever we go.

During this reading plan, we are memorizing our key verse, Isaiah 43:1. This week, we'll continue with the next two lines of the verse.

SEE TIPS FOR MEMORIZING SCRIPTURE ON PAGE 272.

TRUTH

14

ISAIAH 43:1

Now this is what the LORD says—the one who created you, Jacob, and the one who formed you, Israel—"Do not fear, for I have redeemed you; I have called you by your name; you are mine."

SALVATION AND JUDGMENT

ON THAT DAY IT WILL BE SAID, "LOOK, THIS IS OUR GOD; WE HAVE WAITED FOR HIM, AND HE HAS SAVED US. THIS IS THE LORD; WE HAVE WAITED FOR HIM. LET'S REJOICE AND BE GLAD IN HIS SALVATION."

ISAIAH 25:9

DAY 15 — SECTION 1

ISAIAH 24

THE EARTH JUDGED

¹ Look, the LORD is stripping the earth bare
and making it desolate.
He will twist its surface and scatter its inhabitants:
² people and priest alike,
servant and master,
female servant and mistress,
buyer and seller,
lender and borrower,
creditor and debtor.
³ The earth will be stripped completely bare
and will be totally plundered,
for the LORD has spoken this message.
⁴ The earth mourns and withers;
the world wastes away and withers;
the exalted people of the earth waste away.
⁵ The earth is polluted by its inhabitants,
for they have transgressed teachings,
overstepped decrees,
and broken the permanent covenant.
⁶ Therefore a curse has consumed the earth,
and its inhabitants have become guilty;
the earth's inhabitants have been burned,
and only a few survive.
⁷ The new wine mourns;
the vine withers.
All the carousers now groan.
⁸ The joyful tambourines have ceased.
The noise of the jubilant has stopped.
The joyful lyre has ceased.
⁹ They no longer sing and drink wine;
beer is bitter to those who drink it.
¹⁰ The city of chaos is shattered;
every house is closed to entry.
¹¹ In the streets they cry for wine.
All joy grows dark;
earth's rejoicing goes into exile.
¹² Only desolation remains in the city;
its gate has collapsed in ruins.

NOTES

¹³ For this is how it will be on earth
among the nations:
like a harvested olive tree,
like a gleaning after a grape harvest.
¹⁴ They raise their voices, they sing out;
they proclaim in the west
the majesty of the Lord.
¹⁵ Therefore, in the east honor the Lord!
In the coasts and islands of the west
honor the name of the Lord,
the God of Israel.
¹⁶ From the ends of the earth we hear songs:
The Splendor of the Righteous One.
But I said, "I waste away! I waste away!
Woe is me."
The treacherous act treacherously;
the treacherous deal very treacherously.

¹⁷ Panic, pit, and trap await you
who dwell on the earth.
¹⁸ Whoever flees at the sound of panic
will fall into a pit,
and whoever escapes from the pit
will be caught in a trap.
For the floodgates on high are opened,
and the foundations of the earth are shaken.
¹⁹ The earth is completely devastated;
the earth is split open;
the earth is violently shaken.
²⁰ The earth staggers like a drunkard
and sways like a hut.
Earth's rebellion weighs it down,
and it falls, never to rise again.

²¹ On that day the Lord will punish
the army of the heights in the heights
and the kings of the ground on the ground.
²² They will be gathered together
like prisoners in a pit.
They will be confined to a dungeon;
after many days they will be punished.

²³ The moon will be put to shame
and the sun disgraced,
because the Lord of Armies will reign as king
on Mount Zion in Jerusalem,
and he will display his glory
in the presence of his elders.

ISAIAH 25

SALVATION AND JUDGMENT ON THAT DAY

¹ Lord, you are my God;
I will exalt you. I will praise your name,
for you have accomplished wonders,
plans formed long ago, with perfect faithfulness.
² For you have turned the city into a pile of rocks,
a fortified city, into ruins;
the fortress of barbarians is no longer a city;
it will never be rebuilt.
³ Therefore, a strong people will honor you.
The cities of violent nations will fear you.
⁴ For you have been a stronghold for the poor person,
a stronghold for the needy in his distress,
a refuge from storms and a shade from heat.
When the breath of the violent
is like a storm against a wall,
⁵ like heat in a dry land,
you will subdue the uproar of barbarians.
As the shade of a cloud cools the heat of the day,
so he will silence the song of the violent.

⁶ On this mountain,
the Lord of Armies will prepare for all the peoples a feast of
    choice meat,
a feast with aged wine, prime cuts of choice meat, fine vintage wine.
⁷ On this mountain
he will swallow up the burial shroud,
the shroud over all the peoples,
the sheet covering all the nations.
⁸ When he has swallowed up death once and for all,
the Lord God will wipe away the tears

from every face
and remove his people's disgrace
from the whole earth,
for the LORD has spoken.

⁹ On that day it will be said,
"Look, this is our God;
we have waited for him, and he has saved us.
This is the LORD; we have waited for him.
Let's rejoice and be glad in his salvation."
¹⁰ For the LORD's power will rest on this mountain.
But Moab will be trampled in his place
as straw is trampled in a dung pile.

¹¹ He will spread out his arms in the middle of it,
as a swimmer spreads out his arms to swim.
His pride will be brought low,
along with the trickery of his hands.
¹² The high-walled fortress will be brought down,
thrown to the ground, to the dust.

◆ GOING DEEPER

PSALM 30

JOY IN THE MORNING

A psalm; a dedication song for the house. Of David.

¹ I will exalt you, LORD,
because you have lifted me up
and have not allowed my enemies
to triumph over me.
² LORD my God,
I cried to you for help, and you healed me.
³ LORD, you brought me up from Sheol;
you spared me from among those
going down to the Pit.

NOTES

⁴ Sing to the Lord, you his faithful ones,
and praise his holy name.
⁵ For his anger lasts only a moment,
but his favor, a lifetime.
Weeping may stay overnight,
but there is joy in the morning.

⁶ When I was secure, I said,
"I will never be shaken."
⁷ Lord, when you showed your favor,
you made me stand like a strong mountain;
when you hid your face, I was terrified.
⁸ Lord, I called to you;
I sought favor from my Lord:
⁹ "What gain is there in my death,
if I go down to the Pit?
Will the dust praise you?
Will it proclaim your truth?
¹⁰ Lord, listen and be gracious to me;
Lord, be my helper."

¹¹ You turned my lament into dancing; you removed my sackcloth and clothed me with gladness,

¹² so that I can sing to you and not be silent.
Lord my God, I will praise you forever.

HYMN

COME, THOU ALMIGHTY KING

WORDS: ANONYMOUS
MUSIC: FELICE DE GIARDINI

THE SONG OF JUDAH

DAY 16   SECTION 1

ISAIAH 26

THE SONG OF JUDAH

¹ On that day this song will be sung in the land of Judah:

> We have a strong city.
> Salvation is established as walls and ramparts.
> ² Open the gates
> so a righteous nation can come in—
> one that remains faithful.
> ³ You will keep the mind that is dependent on you
> in perfect peace,
> for it is trusting in you.
> ⁴ Trust in the Lord forever,
> because in the Lord, the Lord himself, is an everlasting rock!
> ⁵ For he has humbled those who live in lofty places—
> an inaccessible city.
> He brings it down; he brings it down to the ground;
> he throws it to the dust.
> ⁶ Feet trample it,
> the feet of the humble,
> the steps of the poor.

GOD'S PEOPLE VINDICATED

> ⁷ The path of the righteous is level;
> you clear a straight path for the righteous.
> ⁸ Yes, Lord, we wait for you
> in the path of your judgments.
> Our desire is for your name and renown.
> ⁹ I long for you in the night;
> yes, my spirit within me diligently seeks you,

NOTES

for when your judgments are in the land,
the inhabitants of the world will learn righteousness.
¹⁰ But if the wicked man is shown favor,
he does not learn righteousness.
In a righteous land he acts unjustly
and does not see the majesty of the Lord.
¹¹ Lord, your hand is lifted up to take action,
but they do not see it.
Let them see your zeal for your people
and be put to shame.
Let fire consume your adversaries.
¹² Lord, you will establish peace for us,
for you have also done all our work for us.
¹³ Lord our God, lords other than you have owned us,
but we remember your name alone.

¹⁴ The dead do not live;
departed spirits do not rise up.
Indeed, you have punished and destroyed them;
you have wiped out all memory of them.
¹⁵ You have added to the nation, Lord.
You have added to the nation; you are honored.
You have expanded all the borders of the land.
¹⁶ Lord, they went to you in their distress;
they poured out whispered prayers
because your discipline fell on them.
¹⁷ As a pregnant woman about to give birth
writhes and cries out in her pains,
so we were before you, Lord.
¹⁸ We became pregnant, we writhed in pain;
we gave birth to wind.
We have won no victories on earth,
and the earth's inhabitants have not fallen.

¹⁹ Your dead will live; their bodies will rise.
Awake and sing, you who dwell in the dust!
For you will be covered with the morning dew,
and the earth will bring out the departed spirits.

²⁰ Go, my people, enter your rooms
and close your doors behind you.

Hide for a little while until the wrath has passed.
²¹ For look, the Lord is coming from his place
to punish the inhabitants of the earth for their iniquity.
The earth will reveal the blood shed on it
and will no longer conceal her slain.

◼ GOING DEEPER

LAMENTATIONS 3:19–24

ז ZAYIN

¹⁹ Remember my affliction and my homelessness,
the wormwood and the poison.
²⁰ I continually remember them
and have become depressed.
²¹ Yet I call this to mind,
and therefore I have hope:

ח CHETH

²² Because of the Lord's faithful love
we do not perish,
for his mercies never end.
²³ They are new every morning;
great is your faithfulness!
²⁴ I say, "The Lord is my portion,
therefore I will put my hope in him."

REVELATION 4:9–11

⁹ Whenever the living creatures give glory, honor, and thanks to the one seated on the throne, the one who lives forever and ever, ¹⁰ the twenty-four elders fall down before the one seated on the throne and worship the one who lives forever and ever. They cast their crowns before the throne and say,

¹¹ Our Lord and God,
you are worthy to receive
glory and honor and power,
because you have created all things,
and by your will
they exist and were created.

DAY 17

THE LORD'S VINEYARD

SECTION 1

ISAIAH 27

LEVIATHAN SLAIN

¹ On that day the LORD with his relentless, large, strong sword will bring judgment on Leviathan, the fleeing serpent—Leviathan, the twisting serpent. He will slay the monster that is in the sea.

THE LORD'S VINEYARD

² On that day
sing about a desirable vineyard:
³ I am the LORD, who watches over it
to water it regularly.
So that no one disturbs it,
I watch over it night and day.
⁴ I am not angry.
If only there were thorns and briers for me to battle,
I would trample them
and burn them to the ground.
⁵ Or let it take hold of my strength;
let it make peace with me—
make peace with me.
⁶ In days to come, Jacob will take root.
Israel will blossom and bloom
and fill the whole world with fruit.

⁷ Did the LORD strike Israel
as he struck the one who struck Israel?
Was Israel killed like those killed by the LORD?
⁸ You disputed with Israel
by banishing and driving her away.
He removed her with his severe storm
on the day of the east wind.
⁹ Therefore Jacob's iniquity will be atoned for in this way,
and the result of the removal of his sin will be this:
when he makes all the altar stones
like crushed bits of chalk,
no Asherah poles or incense altars will remain standing.
¹⁰ For the fortified city will be desolate,
pastures deserted and abandoned like a wilderness.
Calves will graze there,
and there they will spread out and strip its branches.

¹¹ When its branches dry out, they will be broken off.
Women will come and make fires with them,
for they are not a people with understanding.
Therefore their Maker will not have compassion on them,
and their Creator will not be gracious to them.

¹² On that day
the Lord will thresh grain from the Euphrates River
as far as the Wadi of Egypt,
and you Israelites will be gathered one by one.
¹³ On that day
a great ram's horn will be blown,
and those lost in the land of Assyria will come,
as well as those dispersed in the land of Egypt;
and they will worship the Lord
at Jerusalem on the holy mountain.

ISAIAH 28

WOE TO SAMARIA

¹ Woe to the majestic crown of Ephraim's drunkards,
and to the fading flower of its beautiful splendor,
which is on the summit above the rich valley.
Woe to those overcome with wine.
² Look, the Lord has a strong and mighty one—
like a devastating hail storm,
like a storm with strong flooding water.
He will bring it across the land with his hand.
³ The majestic crown of Ephraim's drunkards
will be trampled underfoot.
⁴ The fading flower of his beautiful splendor,
which is on the summit above the rich valley,
will be like a ripe fig before the summer harvest.
Whoever sees it will swallow it
while it is still in his hand.
⁵ On that day
the Lord of Armies will become a crown of beauty
and a diadem of splendor
to the remnant of his people,
⁶ a spirit of justice
to the one who sits in judgment,

and strength
to those who repel attacks at the city gate.

⁷ Even these stagger because of wine
and stumble under the influence of beer:
Priest and prophet stagger because of beer.
They are confused by wine.
They stumble because of beer.
They are muddled in their visions.
They stumble in their judgments.
⁸ Indeed, all their tables are covered with vomit;
there is no place without a stench.
⁹ Who is he trying to teach?
Who is he trying to instruct?
Infants just weaned from milk?
Babies removed from the breast?
¹⁰ "Law after law, law after law,
line after line, line after line,
a little here, a little there."
¹¹ For he will speak to this people
with stammering speech
and in a foreign language.
¹² He had said to them,
"This is the place of rest;
let the weary rest;
this is the place of repose."
But they would not listen.

¹³ The word of the Lord will come to them:
"Law after law, law after law,
line after line, line after line,
a little here, a little there,"
so they go stumbling backward,
to be broken, trapped, and captured.

A DEAL WITH DEATH

¹⁴ Therefore hear the word of the Lord, you scoffers
who rule this people in Jerusalem.
¹⁵ For you said, "We have made a covenant with Death,
and we have an agreement with Sheol;
when the overwhelming catastrophe passes through,

it will not touch us,
because we have made falsehood our refuge
and have hidden behind treachery."
¹⁶ Therefore the Lord God said:
"Look, I have laid a stone in Zion,
a tested stone,
a precious cornerstone, a sure foundation;
the one who believes will be unshakable.
¹⁷ And I will make justice the measuring line
and righteousness the mason's level."
Hail will sweep away the false refuge,
and water will flood your hiding place.
¹⁸ Your covenant with Death will be dissolved,
and your agreement with Sheol will not last.
When the overwhelming catastrophe passes through,
you will be trampled.
¹⁹ Every time it passes through,
it will carry you away;
it will pass through every morning—
every day and every night.
Only terror will cause you
to understand the message.
²⁰ Indeed, the bed is too short to stretch out on,
and its cover too small to wrap up in.
²¹ For the Lord will rise up as he did at Mount Perazim.
He will rise in wrath, as at the Valley of Gibeon,
to do his work, his unexpected work,
and to perform his task, his unfamiliar task.
²² So now, do not scoff,
or your shackles will become stronger.
Indeed, I have heard from the Lord God of Armies
a decree of destruction for the whole land.

GOD'S WONDERFUL ADVICE

²³ Listen and hear my voice.
Pay attention and hear what I say.
²⁴ Does the plowman plow every day to plant seed?
Does he continuously break up and cultivate the soil?
²⁵ When he has leveled its surface,
does he not then scatter black cumin and sow cumin?

He plants wheat in rows and barley in plots,
with spelt as their border.
²⁶ His God teaches him order;
he instructs him.
²⁷ Certainly black cumin is not threshed
with a threshing board,
and a cart wheel is not rolled over the cumin.
But black cumin is beaten out with a stick,
and cumin with a rod.
²⁸ Bread grain is crushed,
but is not threshed endlessly.
Though the wheel of the farmer's cart rumbles,
his horses do not crush it.
²⁹ This also comes from the Lord of Armies.
He gives wondrous advice;
he gives great wisdom.

GOING DEEPER

JOHN 15:1–8

THE VINE AND THE BRANCHES

¹ "I am the true vine, and my Father is the gardener. ² Every branch in me that does not produce fruit he removes, and he prunes every branch that produces fruit so that it will produce more fruit. ³ You are already clean because of the word I have spoken to you. ⁴ Remain in me, and I in you. Just as a branch is unable to produce fruit by itself unless it remains on the vine, neither can you unless you remain in me.

> ⁵ I am the vine; you are the branches. The one who remains in me and I in him produces much fruit, because you can do nothing without me.

⁶ If anyone does not remain in me, he is thrown aside like a branch and he withers. They gather them, throw them into the fire, and they are burned. ⁷ If you remain in me and my words remain in you, ask whatever you want and it will be done for you. ⁸ My Father is glorified by this: that you produce much fruit and prove to be my disciples."

THE LORD'S MERCY TO ISRAEL

DAY 18   SECTION 1

ISAIAH 29

WOE TO JERUSALEM

¹ Woe to Ariel, Ariel,
the city where David camped!
Continue year after year;
let the festivals recur.
² I will oppress Ariel,
and there will be mourning and crying,
and she will be to me like an Ariel.
³ I will camp in a circle around you;
I will besiege you with earth ramps,
and I will set up my siege towers against you.
⁴ You will be brought down;
you will speak from the ground,
and your words will come from low in
    the dust.
Your voice will be like that of a spirit from
    the ground;
your speech will whisper from the dust.

⁵ Your many foes will be like fine dust,
and many of the ruthless, like blowing chaff.
Then suddenly, in an instant,
⁶ you will be punished by the LORD of Armies
with thunder, earthquake, and loud noise,
storm, tempest, and a flame of consuming fire.

⁷ All the many nations
going out to battle against Ariel—
all the attackers, the siege works against her,
and those who oppress her—
will then be like a dream, a vision in
    the night.
⁸ It will be like a hungry one who dreams
    he is eating,
then wakes and is still hungry;
and like a thirsty one who dreams he
    is drinking,
then wakes and is still thirsty, longing
    for water.
So it will be for all the many nations
who go to battle against Mount Zion.

⁹ Stop and be astonished;
blind yourselves and be blind!
They are drunk, but not with wine;
they stagger, but not with beer.
¹⁰ For the LORD has poured out on you
an overwhelming urge to sleep;
he has shut your eyes (the prophets)
and covered your heads (the seers).

NOTES

¹¹ For you the entire vision will be like the words of a sealed document. If it is given to one who can read and he is asked to read it, he will say, "I can't read it, because it is sealed." ¹² And if the document is given to one who cannot read and he is asked to read it, he will say, "I can't read."

¹³ The Lord said:

> These people approach me with their speeches
> to honor me with lip-service,
> yet their hearts are far from me,
> and human rules direct their worship of me.
> ¹⁴ Therefore, I will again confound these people
> with wonder after wonder.
> The wisdom of their wise will vanish,
> and the perception of their perceptive will be hidden.
>
> ¹⁵ Woe to those who go to great lengths
> to hide their plans from the Lord.
> They do their works in the dark,
> and say, "Who sees us? Who knows us?"
> ¹⁶ You have turned things around,
> as if the potter were the same as the clay.
> How can what is made say about its maker,
> "He didn't make me"?
> How can what is formed
> say about the one who formed it,
> "He doesn't understand what he's doing"?
>
> ¹⁷ Isn't it true that in just a little while
> Lebanon will become an orchard,
> and the orchard will seem like a forest?
> ¹⁸ On that day the deaf will hear
> the words of a document,
> and out of a deep darkness
> the eyes of the blind will see.
> ¹⁹ The humble will have joy
> after joy in the Lord,
> and the poor people will rejoice
> in the Holy One of Israel.
> ²⁰ For the ruthless one will vanish,
> the scorner will disappear,

and all those who lie in wait with evil intent
will be killed—
²¹ those who, with their speech,
accuse a person of wrongdoing,
who set a trap for the one mediating at the
   city gate
and without cause deprive the righteous
   of justice.

²² Therefore, the Lord who redeemed Abraham says this about the house of Jacob:

Jacob will no longer be ashamed,
and his face will no longer be pale.
²³ For when he sees his children,
the work of my hands within his nation,
they will honor my name,
they will honor the Holy One of Jacob
and stand in awe of the God of Israel.
²⁴ Those who are confused will
   gain understanding,
and those who grumble will
   accept instruction.

ISAIAH 30

CONDEMNATION OF THE EGYPTIAN ALLIANCE

¹ Woe to the rebellious children!
This is the Lord's declaration.
They carry out a plan, but not mine;
they make an alliance,
but against my will,
piling sin on top of sin.
² Without asking my advice
they set out to go down to Egypt
in order to seek shelter under
   Pharaoh's protection
and take refuge in Egypt's shadow.
³ But Pharaoh's protection will become
   your shame,
and refuge in Egypt's shadow
   your humiliation.
⁴ For though his princes are at Zoan
and his messengers reach as far as Hanes,
⁵ everyone will be ashamed
because of a people who can't help.
They are of no benefit, they are no help;
they are good for nothing but shame
   and disgrace.

⁶ A pronouncement concerning the animals of the Negev:

Through a land of trouble and distress,
of lioness and lion,
of viper and flying serpent,
they carry their wealth on the backs
   of donkeys
and their treasures on the humps of camels,
to a people who will not help them.
⁷ Egypt's help is completely worthless;
therefore, I call her:
Rahab Who Just Sits.

⁸ Go now, write it on a tablet in their presence
and inscribe it on a scroll;
it will be for the future,
forever and ever.
⁹ They are a rebellious people,
deceptive children,
children who do not want to listen to the
   Lord's instruction.
¹⁰ They say to the seers, "Do not see,"
and to the prophets,
"Do not prophesy the truth to us.
Tell us flattering things.
Prophesy illusions.
¹¹ Get out of the way!
Leave the pathway.
Rid us of the Holy One of Israel."
¹² Therefore the Holy One of Israel says:

"Because you have rejected this message
and have trusted in oppression and deceit,
and have depended on them,
¹³ this iniquity of yours will be
like a crumbling gap,
a bulge in a high wall
whose collapse will come in an instant—suddenly!
¹⁴ Its collapse will be like the shattering
of a potter's jar, crushed to pieces,
so that not even a fragment of pottery
will be found among its shattered remains—
no fragment large enough to take fire from a hearth
or scoop water from a cistern."
¹⁵ For the Lord God, the Holy One of Israel, has said:
"You will be delivered by returning and resting;
your strength will lie in quiet confidence.
But you are not willing."
¹⁶ You say, "No!
We will escape on horses"—
therefore you will escape!—
and, "We will ride on fast horses"—
but those who pursue you will be faster.
¹⁷ One thousand will flee at the threat of one,
at the threat of five you will flee,
until you remain
like a solitary pole on a mountaintop
or a banner on a hill.

THE LORD'S MERCY TO ISRAEL

¹⁸ Therefore the Lord is waiting to show you mercy,
and is rising up to show you compassion,
for the Lord is a just God.
All who wait patiently for him are happy.

¹⁹ For people will live on Zion in Jerusalem. You will never weep again; he will show favor to you at the sound of your outcry; as soon as he hears, he will answer you. ²⁰ The Lord will give you meager bread and water during oppression, but your Teacher will not hide any longer. Your eyes will see your Teacher, ²¹ and whenever you turn to the right or to the left, your ears will hear this command behind you: "This is the way. Walk in it."

²² Then you will defile your silver-plated idols and your gold-plated images. You will throw them away like menstrual cloths, and call them filth.

²³ Then he will send rain for your seed that you have sown in the ground, and the food, the produce of the ground, will be rich and plentiful. On that day your cattle will graze in open pastures. ²⁴ The oxen and donkeys that work the ground will eat salted fodder scattered with winnowing shovel and fork. ²⁵ Streams flowing with water will be on every high mountain and every raised hill on the day of great slaughter when the towers fall. ²⁶ The moonlight will be as bright as the sunlight, and the sunlight will be seven times brighter—like the light of seven days—on the day that the Lord bandages his people's injuries and heals the wounds he inflicted.

ANNIHILATION OF THE ASSYRIANS

²⁷ Look! The name of the Lord is coming
   from far away,
his anger burning and heavy with smoke.
His lips are full of fury,
and his tongue is like a consuming fire.
²⁸ His breath is like an overflowing torrent
   that rises to the neck.
He comes to sift the nations in a sieve
   of destruction
and to put a bridle on the jaws of the peoples
   to lead them astray.
²⁹ Your singing will be like that
   on the night of a holy festival,
and your heart will rejoice
like one who walks to the music of a flute,
going up to the mountain of the Lord,
   to the Rock of Israel.
³⁰ And the Lord will make the splendor of
   his voice heard
and reveal his arm striking in angry wrath
and a flame of consuming fire,
   in driving rain, a torrent, and hailstones.
³¹ Assyria will be shattered by the voice of
   the Lord.
He will strike with a rod.
³² And every stroke of the appointed staff
that the Lord brings down on him
will be to the sound of tambourines
   and lyres;
he will fight against him with
   brandished weapons.
³³ Indeed! Topheth has been ready
for the king for a long time.
Its funeral pyre is deep and wide,
with plenty of fire and wood.
The breath of the Lord, like a torrent of
   burning sulfur,
kindles it.

◆ GOING DEEPER

PSALM 20:6-9

⁶ Now I know that the Lord gives victory to
   his anointed;
he will answer him from his holy heaven
with mighty victories from his right hand.
⁷ Some take pride in chariots, and others
   in horses,
but we take pride in the name of the Lord
   our God.
⁸ They collapse and fall,
but we rise and stand firm.
⁹ Lord, give victory to the king!
May he answer us on the day that we call.

ROMANS 9:20-26

²⁰ On the contrary, who are you, a human being, to talk back to God? Will what is formed

say to the one who formed it, "Why did you make me like this?" ²¹ Or has the potter no right over the clay, to make from the same lump one piece of pottery for honor and another for dishonor? ²² And what if God, wanting to display his wrath and to make his power known, endured with much patience objects of wrath prepared for destruction?

²³ And what if he did this to make known the riches of his glory on objects of mercy that he prepared beforehand for glory—

²⁴ on us, the ones he also called, not only from the Jews but also from the Gentiles? ²⁵ As it also says in Hosea,

> I will call Not My People, My People,
> and she who is Unloved, Beloved.
> ²⁶ And it will be in the place where they were told,
> you are not my people,
> there they will be called sons of the living God.

NOTES

DAY 19   SECTION 1

THE RIGHTEOUS KINGDOM ANNOUNCED

ISAIAH 31

THE LORD, THE ONLY HELP

¹ Woe to those who go down to Egypt for help
and who depend on horses!
They trust in the abundance of chariots
and in the large number of horsemen.
They do not look to the Holy One of Israel,
and they do not seek the Lord.
² But he also is wise and brings disaster.
He does not go back on what he says;
he will rise up against the house of the wicked
and against the allies of evildoers.
³ Egyptians are men, not God;
their horses are flesh, not spirit.
When the Lord raises his hand to strike,
the helper will stumble
and the one who is helped will fall;
both will perish together.

⁴ For this is what the LORD said to me:

> As a lion or young lion growls over its prey
> when a band of shepherds is called out against it,
> and it is not terrified by their shouting
> or subdued by their noise,
> so the LORD of Armies will come down
> to fight on Mount Zion
> and on its hill.
>
> ⁵ Like hovering birds,
> so the LORD of Armies will protect Jerusalem;
> by protecting it, he will rescue it;
> by passing over it, he will deliver it.

⁶ Return to the one the Israelites have greatly rebelled against. ⁷ For on that day, every one of you will reject the worthless idols of silver and gold that your own hands have sinfully made.

> ⁸ Then Assyria will fall,
> but not by human sword;
> a sword will devour him,
> but not one made by man.
> He will flee from the sword;
> his young men will be put to forced labor.
>
> ⁹ His rock will pass away because of fear,
> and his officers will be afraid because of the signal flag.

This is the LORD's declaration—whose fire is in Zion and whose furnace is in Jerusalem.

ISAIAH 32

THE RIGHTEOUS KINGDOM ANNOUNCED

> ¹ Indeed, a king will reign righteously,
> and rulers will rule justly.
>
> ² Each will be like a shelter from the wind,
> a refuge from the rain,

like flowing streams in a dry land
and the shade of a massive rock in an
    arid land.
³ Then the eyes of those who see will not
    be closed,
and the ears of those who hear will listen.
⁴ The reckless mind will gain knowledge,
and the stammering tongue will speak clearly
    and fluently.
⁵ A fool will no longer be called a noble,
nor a scoundrel said to be important.
⁶ For a fool speaks foolishness
and his mind plots iniquity.
He lives in a godless way
and speaks falsely about the LORD.
He leaves the hungry empty
and deprives the thirsty of drink.

⁷ The scoundrel's weapons are destructive;
he hatches plots to destroy the needy
    with lies,
even when the poor person says what is right.
⁸ But a noble person plans noble things;
he stands up for noble causes.
⁹ Stand up, you complacent women;
listen to me.
Pay attention to what I say,
you overconfident daughters.
¹⁰ In a little more than a year
you overconfident ones will shudder,
for the grapes will fail
and the harvest will not come.
¹¹ Shudder, you complacent ones;
tremble, you overconfident ones!
Strip yourselves bare
and put sackcloth around your waists.
¹² Beat your breasts in mourning
for the delightful fields and the fruitful vines,
¹³ for the ground of my people
growing thorns and briers,
indeed, for every joyous house in the
    jubilant city.

¹⁴ For the palace will be deserted,
the busy city abandoned.
The hill and the watchtower will become
barren places forever,
the joy of wild donkeys,
and a pasture for flocks,
¹⁵ until the Spirit from on high is poured out
    on us.
Then the desert will become an orchard,
and the orchard will seem like a forest.
¹⁶ Then justice will inhabit the wilderness,
and righteousness will dwell in the orchard.

¹⁷ The result of righteousness will be peace;
the effect of righteousness
will be quiet confidence forever.
¹⁸ Then my people will dwell in a
    peaceful place,
in safe and secure dwellings.
¹⁹ But hail will level the forest,
and the city will sink into the depths.
²⁰ You will be happy as you sow seed
beside abundant water,
and as you let oxen and donkeys range freely.

GOING DEEPER

PSALM 91

THE PROTECTION OF THE MOST HIGH

¹ The one who lives under the protection of the
    Most High
dwells in the shadow of the Almighty.

² I will say concerning the LORD, who is my
    refuge and my fortress,
my God in whom I trust:
³ He himself will rescue you from the bird trap,
from the destructive plague.
⁴ He will cover you with his feathers;
you will take refuge under his wings.

His faithfulness will be a protective shield.
⁵ You will not fear the terror of the night,
the arrow that flies by day,
⁶ the plague that stalks in darkness,
or the pestilence that ravages at noon.
⁷ Though a thousand fall at your side
and ten thousand at your right hand,
the pestilence will not reach you.
⁸ You will only see it with your eyes
and witness the punishment of the wicked.

⁹ Because you have made the
   Lord—my refuge,
the Most High—your dwelling place,
¹⁰ no harm will come to you;

no plague will come near your tent.
¹¹ For he will give his angels orders concerning you,
to protect you in all your ways.
¹² They will support you with their hands
so that you will not strike your foot against a stone.
¹³ You will tread on the lion and the cobra;
you will trample the young lion and the serpent.

¹⁴ Because he has his heart set on me,
I will deliver him;
I will protect him because he knows my name.
¹⁵ When he calls out to me, I will answer him;
I will be with him in trouble.
I will rescue him and give him honor.
¹⁶ I will satisfy him with a long life
and show him my salvation.

WEEK THREE
RESPONSE

USE THE FOLLOWING WORKSHEET TO HELP YOU REFLECT ON THIS WEEK'S READING.

Places or people the prophecies in this week's reading were directed toward:

An encouraging or challenging verse:

Isaiah :

A question to ponder and investigate:

Descriptive details about God and His people:

God

His People

How God's people were called to respond:

Specific sins revealed or warnings given:

GOD'S HOLINESS

How was God's holiness demonstrated in this week's reading?

Circle one expression of His holiness in your answer above that stands out to you. How might trusting in this aspect of God strengthen your faith this Lenten season?

THE PEOPLE'S SIN

Review the sins that you listed on the previous page and consider how some of them may be present in your own life, even if they are expressed in different ways. Circle one that stands out to you and then use this space to reflect on the ways this sin appears in your own life.

HOPE FOR SALVATION THROUGH GOD

God responds to His people's sin and rebellion with a promise to save and restore them. Looking back on this week's reading, highlight or underline some of God's promises to His people.

Having reflected on God's holiness and the reality of sin, how do these messages of hope encourage you as you journey through this season of Lent?

DAY 20

GRACE DAY

SECTION 1

Take this day to catch up on your reading, pray, and rest in the presence of the Lord.

OUR LORD AND GOD, YOU ARE WORTHY TO RECEIVE GLORY AND HONOR AND POWER, BECAUSE YOU HAVE CREATED ALL THINGS, AND BY YOUR WILL THEY EXIST AND WERE CREATED.

REVELATION 4:11

WEEKLY

DAY ———————

Scripture is God breathed and true. When we memorize it, we carry His Word with us wherever we go.

During this reading plan, we are memorizing our key verse, Isaiah 43:1. This week, we'll continue with the fourth line of the verse.

SEE TIPS FOR MEMORIZING SCRIPTURE ON PAGE 272.

─────────── 21   TRUTH

ISAIAH 43:1

Now this is what the Lord
says—the one who created you,
Jacob, and the one who formed
you, Israel—"<u>Do not fear, for I
have redeemed you</u>; I have called
you by your name; you are mine."

THE LORD RISES UP

―――

"NOW I WILL RISE UP," SAYS THE
LORD. "NOW I WILL LIFT MYSELF UP.
NOW I WILL BE EXALTED."

ISAIAH 33:10

DAY 22   SECTION 1

ISAIAH 33

THE LORD RISES UP

¹ Woe, you destroyer never destroyed,
you traitor never betrayed!
When you have finished destroying,
you will be destroyed.
When you have finished betraying,
they will betray you.
² Lord, be gracious to us! We wait for you.
Be our strength every morning
and our salvation in time of trouble.
³ The peoples flee at the thunderous noise;
the nations scatter when you rise in your majesty.
⁴ Your spoil will be gathered as locusts are gathered;
people will swarm over it like an infestation of locusts.
⁵ The Lord is exalted, for he dwells on high;
he has filled Zion with justice and righteousness.
⁶ There will be times of security for you—
a storehouse of salvation, wisdom, and knowledge.
The fear of the Lord is Zion's treasure.
⁷ Listen! Their warriors cry loudly in the streets;
the messengers of peace weep bitterly.

⁸ The highways are deserted;
travel has ceased.
An agreement has been broken,
cities despised,
and human life disregarded.
⁹ The land mourns and withers;
Lebanon is ashamed and wilted.
Sharon is like a desert;
Bashan and Carmel shake off their leaves.
¹⁰ "Now I will rise up," says the Lord.
"Now I will lift myself up.
Now I will be exalted.
¹¹ You will conceive chaff;
you will give birth to stubble.
Your breath is fire that will consume you.
¹² The peoples will be burned to ashes,
like thorns cut down and burned in a fire.

NOTES

¹³ You who are far off, hear what I have done;
you who are near, know my strength."
¹⁴ The sinners in Zion are afraid;
trembling seizes the ungodly:
"Who among us can dwell with a consuming fire?
Who among us can dwell with ever-burning flames?"
¹⁵ The one who lives righteously
and speaks rightly,
who refuses profit from extortion,
whose hand never takes a bribe,
who stops his ears from listening to murderous plots
and shuts his eyes against evil schemes—
¹⁶ he will dwell on the heights;
his refuge will be the rocky fortresses,
his food provided, his water assured.

¹⁷ Your eyes will see the King in his beauty; you will see a vast land.

¹⁸ Your mind will meditate on the past terror:
"Where is the accountant?
Where is the tribute collector?
Where is the one who spied out our defenses?"
¹⁹ You will no longer see the barbarians,
a people whose speech is difficult to comprehend—
who stammer in a language that is not understood.
²⁰ Look at Zion, the city of our festival times.
Your eyes will see Jerusalem,
a peaceful pasture, a tent that does not wander;
its tent pegs will not be pulled up
nor will any of its cords be loosened.
²¹ For the majestic one, our Lord, will be there,
a place of rivers and broad streams
where ships that are rowed will not go,
and majestic vessels will not pass.
²² For the Lord is our Judge,
the Lord is our Lawgiver,
the Lord is our King.
He will save us.

²³ Your ropes are slack;
they cannot hold the base of the mast
or spread out the flag.
Then abundant spoil will be divided,
the lame will plunder it,
²⁴ and none there will say, "I am sick."
The people who dwell there
will be forgiven their iniquity.

ISAIAH 34

THE JUDGMENT OF THE NATIONS

¹ You nations, come here and listen;
you peoples, pay attention!
Let the earth and all that fills it hear,
the world and all that comes from it.
² The Lord is angry with all the nations,
furious with all their armies.
He will set them apart for destruction,
giving them over to slaughter.
³ Their slain will be thrown out,
and the stench of their corpses will rise;
the mountains will flow with their blood.
⁴ All the stars in the sky will dissolve.
The sky will roll up like a scroll,
and its stars will all wither
as leaves wither on the vine,
and foliage on the fig tree.

THE JUDGMENT OF EDOM

⁵ When my sword has drunk its fill in the heavens,
it will then come down on Edom
and on the people I have set apart for destruction.
⁶ The Lord's sword is covered with blood.
It drips with fat,
with the blood of lambs and goats,
with the fat of the kidneys of rams.
For the Lord has a sacrifice in Bozrah,
a great slaughter in the land of Edom.

NOTES

⁷ The wild oxen will be struck down with them,
and young bulls with the mighty bulls.
Their land will be soaked with blood,
and their soil will be saturated with fat.
⁸ For the Lord has a day of vengeance,
a time of paying back Edom
for its hostility against Zion.
⁹ Edom's streams will be turned into pitch,
her soil into sulfur;
her land will become burning pitch.
¹⁰ It will never go out—day or night.
Its smoke will go up forever.
It will be desolate, from generation to generation;
no one will pass through it forever and ever.
¹¹ Eagle owls and herons will possess it,
and long-eared owls and ravens will dwell there.
The Lord will stretch out a measuring line
and a plumb line over her
for her destruction and chaos.
¹² No nobles will be left to proclaim a king,
and all her princes will come to nothing.
¹³ Her palaces will be overgrown with thorns;
her fortified cities, with thistles and briers.
She will become a dwelling for jackals,
an abode for ostriches.
¹⁴ The desert creatures will meet hyenas,
and one wild goat will call to another.
Indeed, the night birds will stay there
and will find a resting place.
¹⁵ Sand partridges will make their nests there;
they will lay and hatch their eggs
and will gather their broods under their shadows.
Indeed, the birds of prey will gather there,
each with its mate.
¹⁶ Search and read the scroll of the Lord:
Not one of them will be missing,
none will be lacking its mate,
because he has ordered it by my mouth,
and he will gather them by his Spirit.

¹⁷ He has cast the lot for them;
his hand allotted their portion with a measuring line.
They will possess it forever;
they will dwell in it from generation to generation.

GOING DEEPER

ZECHARIAH 10:6

"I will strengthen the house of Judah
and deliver the house of Joseph.
I will restore them
because I have compassion on them,
and they will be
as though I had never rejected them.

For I am the LORD their God,
and I will answer them."

ROMANS 5:8-11

⁸ But God proves his own love for us in that while we were still sinners, Christ died for us. ⁹ How much more then, since we have now been justified by his blood, will we be saved through him from wrath. ¹⁰ For if, while we were enemies, we were reconciled to God through the death of his Son, then how much more, having been reconciled, will we be saved by his life. ¹¹ And not only that, but we also boast in God through our Lord Jesus Christ, through whom we have now received this reconciliation.

THE RANSOMED RETURN

DAY 23   SECTION 1

ISAIAH 35

THE RANSOMED RETURN TO ZION

¹ The wilderness and the dry land will be glad;
the desert will rejoice and blossom like a wildflower.
² It will blossom abundantly
and will also rejoice with joy and singing.
The glory of Lebanon will be given to it,
the splendor of Carmel and Sharon.
They will see the glory of the Lord,
the splendor of our God.
³ Strengthen the weak hands,
steady the shaking knees!
⁴ Say to the cowardly:
"Be strong; do not fear!
Here is your God; vengeance is coming.
God's retribution is coming; he will save you."
⁵ Then the eyes of the blind will be opened,
and the ears of the deaf unstopped.

NOTES

⁶ Then the lame will leap like a deer,
and the tongue of the mute will sing for joy,
for water will gush in the wilderness,
and streams in the desert;
⁷ the parched ground will become a pool,
and the thirsty land, springs.
In the haunt of jackals, in their lairs,
there will be grass, reeds, and papyrus.
⁸ A road will be there and a way;
it will be called the Holy Way.
The unclean will not travel on it,
but it will be for the one who walks the path.
Fools will not wander on it.
⁹ There will be no lion there,
and no vicious beast will go up on it;
they will not be found there.
But the redeemed will walk on it,
¹⁰ and the ransomed of the Lord will return
and come to Zion with singing,
crowned with unending joy.
Joy and gladness will overtake them,
and sorrow and sighing will flee.

ISAIAH 36

SENNACHERIB'S INVASION

¹ In the fourteenth year of King Hezekiah, King Sennacherib of Assyria attacked all the fortified cities of Judah and captured them. ² Then the king of Assyria sent his royal spokesman, along with a massive army, from Lachish to King Hezekiah at Jerusalem. The Assyrian stood near the conduit of the upper pool, by the road to Launderer's Field. ³ Eliakim son of Hilkiah, who was in charge of the palace, Shebna the court secretary, and Joah son of Asaph, the court historian, came out to him.

⁴ The royal spokesman said to them, "Tell Hezekiah:

The great king, the king of Assyria, says this: What are you relying on? ⁵ You think mere words are strategy and strength for war. Who are you now relying on that you have rebelled against me? ⁶ Look, you are relying on Egypt, that splintered reed of a staff that will pierce the hand of anyone who grabs it and leans on it. This is how Pharaoh king of Egypt is to all who rely on him. ⁷ Suppose you say to me, 'We rely on the Lord our God.' Isn't he the one whose high places and altars Hezekiah has removed, saying to Judah and Jerusalem, 'You are to worship at this altar'?

⁸ "Now make a deal with my master, the king of Assyria. I'll give you two thousand horses if you're able to supply riders for them! ⁹ How then can you drive back a single officer among the least of my master's servants? How can you rely on Egypt for chariots and horsemen? ¹⁰ Have I attacked this land to destroy it without the Lord's approval? The Lord said to me, 'Attack this land and destroy it.'"

¹¹ Then Eliakim, Shebna, and Joah said to the royal spokesman, "Please speak to your servants in Aramaic, since we understand it. Don't speak to us in Hebrew within earshot of the people who are on the wall."

¹² But the royal spokesman replied, "Has my master sent me to speak these words to your master and to you, and not to the men who are sitting on the wall, who are destined with you to eat their own excrement and drink their own urine?"

¹³ Then the royal spokesman stood and called out loudly in Hebrew:

Listen to the words of the great king, the king of Assyria! ¹⁴ This is what the king says: "Don't let Hezekiah deceive you, for he cannot rescue you. ¹⁵ Don't let Hezekiah persuade you to rely on the Lord, saying, 'The Lord will certainly rescue us! This city will not be handed over to the king of Assyria.'"

¹⁶ Don't listen to Hezekiah, for this is what the king of Assyria says: "Make peace with me and surrender to me. Then every one of you may eat from his own vine and his own fig tree and drink water from his own cistern ¹⁷ until I come and take you away to a land like your own land—a land of grain and new wine, a land of bread and vineyards. ¹⁸ Beware that Hezekiah does not mislead you by saying, 'The Lord will rescue us.' Has any one of the gods of the nations rescued his land from the power of the king of Assyria? ¹⁹ Where are the gods of Hamath and Arpad? Where are the gods of Sepharvaim? Have they rescued Samaria from my power? ²⁰ Who among all the gods of these lands ever rescued his land from my power? So will the Lord rescue Jerusalem from my power?"

NOTES

²¹ But they kept silent; they didn't say anything, for the king's command was, "Don't answer him." ²² Then Eliakim son of Hilkiah, who was in charge of the palace, Shebna the court secretary, and Joah son of Asaph, the court historian, came to Hezekiah with their clothes torn and reported to him the words of the royal spokesman.

GOING DEEPER

ZEPHANIAH 3:14-20

¹⁴ Sing for joy, Daughter Zion;
shout loudly, Israel!
Be glad and celebrate with all your heart,
Daughter Jerusalem!
¹⁵ The Lord has removed your punishment;
he has turned back your enemy.
The King of Israel, the Lord, is among you;
you need no longer fear harm.
¹⁶ On that day it will be said to Jerusalem:
"Do not fear;
Zion, do not let your hands grow weak.
¹⁷ The Lord your God is among you,
a warrior who saves.
He will rejoice over you with gladness.
He will be quiet in his love.
He will delight in you with singing."

¹⁸ I will gather those who have been driven
from the appointed festivals;
they will be a tribute from you
and a reproach on her.
¹⁹ Yes, at that time
I will deal with all who oppress you.
I will save the lame and gather the outcasts;
I will make those who were disgraced
throughout the earth
receive praise and fame.
²⁰ At that time I will bring you back,
yes, at the time I will gather you.

I will give you fame and praise
among all the peoples of the earth,
when I restore your fortunes before your eyes.
The LORD has spoken.

2 CORINTHIANS 7:9-12

⁹ I now rejoice, not because you were grieved, but because your grief led to repentance. For you were grieved as God willed, so that you didn't experience any loss from us. ¹⁰ For godly grief produces a repentance that leads to salvation without regret, but worldly grief produces death. ¹¹ For consider how much diligence this very thing—this grieving as God wills—has produced in you: what a desire to clear yourselves, what indignation, what fear, what deep longing, what zeal, what justice! In every way you showed yourselves to be pure in this matter. ¹² So even though I wrote to you, it was not because of the one who did wrong, or because of the one who was wronged, but in order that your devotion to us might be made plain to you in the sight of God.

NOTES

HEZEKIAH'S PRAYER

DAY 24　　　　　　　　　　　　　　　　　　　　　　　　SECTION 1

ISAIAH 37

HEZEKIAH SEEKS ISAIAH'S COUNSEL

¹ When King Hezekiah heard their report, he tore his clothes, covered himself with sackcloth, and went to the LORD's temple. ² He sent Eliakim, who was in charge of the palace, Shebna the court secretary, and the leading priests, who were covered with sackcloth, to the prophet Isaiah son of Amoz. ³ They said to him, "This is what Hezekiah says: 'Today is a day of distress, rebuke, and disgrace. It is as if children have come to the point of birth, and there is no strength to deliver them. ⁴ Perhaps the LORD your God will hear all the words of the royal spokesman, whom his master the king of Assyria sent to mock the living God, and will rebuke him for the words that the LORD your God has heard. Therefore offer a prayer for the surviving remnant.'"

⁵ So the servants of King Hezekiah went to Isaiah, ⁶ who said to them, "Tell your master, 'The LORD says this: Don't be afraid because of the words you have heard, with which the king of Assyria's attendants have blasphemed me. ⁷ I am about to put a spirit in him and he will hear a rumor and return to his own land, where I will cause him to fall by the sword.'"

SENNACHERIB'S LETTER

⁸ When the royal spokesman heard that the king of Assyria had pulled out of Lachish, he left and found him fighting against Libnah. ⁹ The king had heard concerning King Tirhakah of Cush, "He has set out to fight against you." So when he heard this, he sent messengers to Hezekiah, saying, ¹⁰ "Say this to King Hezekiah of Judah: 'Don't let your God, on whom you rely, deceive you by promising that Jerusalem won't be handed over to the king of Assyria. ¹¹ Look, you have heard what the kings of Assyria have done to all the countries: they completely destroyed them. Will you be rescued? ¹² Did the gods of the nations that my predecessors destroyed rescue them—Gozan, Haran, Rezeph, and the Edenites in Telassar? ¹³ Where is the king of Hamath, the king of Arpad, the king of the city of Sepharvaim, Hena, or Ivvah?'"

HEZEKIAH'S PRAYER

¹⁴ Hezekiah took the letter from the messengers' hands, read it, then went up to the LORD's temple and spread it out before the LORD. ¹⁵ Then Hezekiah prayed to the LORD:

¹⁶ Lord of Armies, God of Israel, enthroned between the cherubim, you are God—you alone—of all the kingdoms of the earth. You made the heavens and the earth. ¹⁷ Listen closely, Lord, and hear; open your eyes, Lord, and see. Hear all the words that Sennacherib has sent to mock the living God. ¹⁸ Lord, it is true that the kings of Assyria have devastated all these countries and their lands. ¹⁹ They have thrown their gods into the fire, for they were not gods but made from wood and stone by human hands. So they have destroyed them. ²⁰ Now, Lord our God, save us from his power so that all the kingdoms of the earth may know that you, Lord, are God—you alone.

GOD'S ANSWER THROUGH ISAIAH

²¹ Then Isaiah son of Amoz sent a message to Hezekiah: "The Lord, the God of Israel, says, 'Because you prayed to me about King Sennacherib of Assyria, ²² this is the word the Lord has spoken against him:

Virgin Daughter Zion
despises you and scorns you;
Daughter Jerusalem shakes her head
behind your back.
²³ Who is it you have mocked and blasphemed?
Against whom have you raised your voice
and lifted your eyes in pride?
Against the Holy One of Israel!
²⁴ You have mocked the Lord through your servants.
You have said, "With my many chariots
I have gone up to the heights of the mountains,
to the far recesses of Lebanon.
I cut down its tallest cedars,
its choice cypress trees.
I came to its distant heights,
its densest forest.
²⁵ I dug wells and drank water in foreign lands.
I dried up all the streams of Egypt
with the soles of my feet."

²⁶ Have you not heard?
I designed it long ago;
I planned it in days gone by.
I have now brought it to pass,

and you have crushed fortified cities
into piles of rubble.
²⁷ Their inhabitants have become powerless,
dismayed, and ashamed.
They are plants of the field,
tender grass,
grass on the rooftops,
blasted by the east wind.

²⁸ But I know your sitting down,
your going out and your coming in,
and your raging against me.
²⁹ Because your raging against me
and your arrogance have reached my ears,
I will put my hook in your nose
and my bit in your mouth;
I will make you go back
the way you came.

³⁰ "'This will be the sign for you: This year you will eat what grows on its own, and in the second year what grows from that. But in the third year sow and reap, plant vineyards and eat their fruit. ³¹ The surviving remnant of the house of Judah will again take root downward and bear fruit upward. ³² For a remnant will go out from Jerusalem, and survivors from Mount Zion. The zeal of the Lord of Armies will accomplish this.'

³³ "Therefore, this is what the Lord says about the king of Assyria:

He will not enter this city,
shoot an arrow here,
come before it with a shield,
or build up a siege ramp against it.
³⁴ He will go back
the way he came,
and he will not enter this city.

This is the Lord's declaration.

³⁵ I will defend this city and rescue it
for my sake
and for the sake of my servant David."

DEFEAT AND DEATH OF SENNACHERIB

³⁶ Then the angel of the Lord went out and struck down one hundred eighty-five thousand in the camp of the Assyrians. When the people got up the next morning, there were all the dead bodies! ³⁷ So King Sennacherib of Assyria broke camp and left. He returned home and lived in Nineveh.

³⁸ One day, while he was worshiping in the temple of his god Nisroch, his sons Adrammelech and Sharezer struck him down with the sword and escaped to the land of Ararat. Then his son Esar-haddon became king in his place.

ISAIAH 38

HEZEKIAH'S ILLNESS AND RECOVERY

¹ In those days Hezekiah became terminally ill. The prophet Isaiah son of Amoz came and said to him, "This is what the Lord says: 'Set your house in order, for you are about to die; you will not recover.'"

² Then Hezekiah turned his face to the wall and prayed to the Lord. ³ He said, "Please, Lord, remember how I have walked before you faithfully and wholeheartedly, and have done what pleases you." And Hezekiah wept bitterly.

⁴ Then the word of the Lord came to Isaiah: ⁵ "Go and tell Hezekiah, 'This is what the Lord

God of your ancestor David says: I have heard your prayer; I have seen your tears. Look, I am going to add fifteen years to your life. ⁶ And I will rescue you and this city from the grasp of the king of Assyria; I will defend this city. ⁷ This is the sign to you from the LORD that he will do what he has promised: ⁸ I am going to make the sun's shadow that goes down on the stairway of Ahaz go back by ten steps.'" So the sun's shadow went back the ten steps it had descended.

⁹ A poem by King Hezekiah of Judah after he had been sick and had recovered from his illness:

¹⁰ I said: In the prime of my life
I must go to the gates of Sheol;
I am deprived of the rest of my years.
¹¹ I said: I will never see the LORD,
the LORD in the land of the living;
I will not look on humanity any longer
with the inhabitants of what is passing away.
¹² My dwelling is plucked up and removed from me
like a shepherd's tent.
I have rolled up my life like a weaver;
he cuts me off from the loom.
By nightfall you make an end of me.
¹³ I thought until the morning:
He will break all my bones like a lion.
By nightfall you make an end of me.
¹⁴ I chirp like a swallow or a crane;
I moan like a dove.
My eyes grow weak looking upward.
Lord, I am oppressed; support me.

¹⁵ What can I say?
He has spoken to me,
and he himself has done it.
I walk along slowly all my years
because of the bitterness of my soul.
¹⁶ Lord, by such things people live,
and in every one of them my spirit finds life;
you have restored me to health
and let me live.

¹⁷ Indeed, it was for my own well-being
that I had such intense bitterness;
but your love has delivered me
from the Pit of destruction,
for you have thrown all my sins behind
   your back.
¹⁸ For Sheol cannot thank you;
Death cannot praise you.
Those who go down to the Pit
cannot hope for your faithfulness.
¹⁹ The living, only the living can thank you,
as I do today;
a father will make your faithfulness known
   to children.
²⁰ The Lord is ready to save me;
we will play stringed instruments
all the days of our lives
at the house of the Lord.

²¹ Now Isaiah had said, "Let them take a lump of pressed figs and apply it to his infected skin, so that he may recover." ²² And Hezekiah asked, "What is the sign that I will go up to the Lord's temple?"

ISAIAH 39

HEZEKIAH'S FOLLY

¹ At that time Merodach-baladan son of Baladan, king of Babylon, sent letters and a gift to Hezekiah since he heard that he had been sick and had recovered. ² Hezekiah was pleased with the letters, and he showed the envoys his treasure house—the silver, the gold, the spices, and the precious oil—and all his armory, and everything that was found in his treasuries. There was nothing in his palace and in all his realm that Hezekiah did not show them.

³ Then the prophet Isaiah came to King Hezekiah and asked him, "What did these men say, and where did they come to you from?"

Hezekiah replied, "They came to me from a distant country, from Babylon."

⁴ Isaiah asked, "What have they seen in your palace?"

Hezekiah answered, "They have seen everything in my palace. There isn't anything in my treasuries that I didn't show them."

⁵ Then Isaiah said to Hezekiah, "Hear the word of the Lord of Armies: ⁶ 'Look, the days are coming when everything in your palace and all that your predecessors have stored up until today will be carried off to Babylon; nothing will be left,' says the Lord. ⁷ 'Some of your descendants—who come from you, whom you father—will be taken away, and they will become eunuchs in the palace of the king of Babylon.'"

⁸ Then Hezekiah said to Isaiah, "The word of the Lord that you have spoken is good," for he thought: There will be peace and security during my lifetime.

♥ GOING DEEPER

PSALM 2

CORONATION OF THE SON

¹ Why do the nations rage
and the peoples plot in vain?
² The kings of the earth take their stand,
and the rulers conspire together

against the Lord and his Anointed One:
³ "Let's tear off their chains
and throw their ropes off of us."

⁴ The one enthroned in heaven laughs;
the Lord ridicules them.
⁵ Then he speaks to them in his anger
and terrifies them in his wrath:
⁶ "I have installed my king
on Zion, my holy mountain."

⁷ I will declare the Lord's decree.
He said to me, "You are my Son;
today I have become your Father.
⁸ Ask of me,
and I will make the nations your inheritance
and the ends of the earth your possession.
⁹ You will break them with an iron scepter;
you will shatter them like pottery."

¹⁰ So now, kings, be wise;
receive instruction, you judges of the earth.
¹¹ Serve the Lord with reverential awe
and rejoice with trembling.
¹² Pay homage to the Son or he will be angry
and you will perish in your rebellion,
for his anger may ignite at any moment.
All who take refuge in him are happy.

NOTES

SECTION TWO

SALVATION AND SOLACE

ISAIAH 40–55

Isaiah 40-55 is widely considered to be a set of prophecies for a nation in exile. The judgment God spoke about in Isaiah 1-39 came about, and Isaiah 40-55 depicts God's people in captivity in Babylon. This section is mainly written as poetic narrative, a writing style that builds images to communicate God physically and spiritually calling His people out of exile.

Though God judged His disobedient nation, **He also had a plan to save His people and cleanse them of their sin.** His plan was revealed through the rescue that the nation of Judah experienced as they returned to Jerusalem after their exile in Babylon. We see a promised salvation for all people through the promise of a coming Suffering Servant–the ultimate source of comfort and rescue for His people.

DAY 25   SECTION 2

GOD'S PEOPLE COMFORTED

ISAIAH 40

GOD'S PEOPLE COMFORTED

¹ "Comfort, comfort my people,"
says your God.
² "Speak tenderly to Jerusalem,
and announce to her
that her time of hard service is over,
her iniquity has been pardoned,
and she has received from the Lord's hand
double for all her sins."

³ A voice of one crying out:

Prepare the way of the Lord in the wilderness;
make a straight highway for our God in the desert.
⁴ Every valley will be lifted up,
and every mountain and hill will be leveled;
the uneven ground will become smooth
and the rough places, a plain.
⁵ And the glory of the Lord will appear,
and all humanity together will see it,
for the mouth of the Lord has spoken.

⁶ A voice was saying, "Cry out!"
Another said, "What should I cry out?"
"All humanity is grass,
and all its goodness is like the flower of the field.
⁷ The grass withers, the flowers fade
when the breath of the Lord blows on them;
indeed, the people are grass.
⁸ The grass withers, the flowers fade,
but the word of our God remains forever."

⁹ Zion, herald of good news,
go up on a high mountain.
Jerusalem, herald of good news,
raise your voice loudly.
Raise it, do not be afraid!
Say to the cities of Judah,
"Here is your God!"
¹⁰ See, the Lord God comes with strength,
and his power establishes his rule.
His wages are with him,
and his reward accompanies him.
¹¹ He protects his flock like a shepherd;
he gathers the lambs in his arms
and carries them in the fold of his garment.
He gently leads those that are nursing.

¹² Who has measured the waters in the hollow of his hand
or marked off the heavens with the span of his hand?
Who has gathered the dust of the earth in a measure
or weighed the mountains on a balance
and the hills on the scales?
¹³ Who has directed the Spirit of the Lord,
or who gave him counsel?
¹⁴ Who did he consult?
Who gave him understanding
and taught him the paths of justice?
Who taught him knowledge
and showed him the way of understanding?
¹⁵ Look, the nations are like a drop in a bucket;
they are considered as a speck of dust on the scales;
he lifts up the islands like fine dust.
¹⁶ Lebanon's cedars are not enough for fuel,

NOTES

or its animals enough for a burnt offering.
¹⁷ All the nations are as nothing before him;
they are considered by him
as empty nothingness.

¹⁸ With whom will you compare God?
What likeness will you set up for comparison
  with him?
¹⁹ An idol?—something that a smelter casts
and a metalworker plates with gold
and makes silver chains for?
²⁰ A poor person contributes wood for
  a pedestal
that will not rot.
He looks for a skilled craftsman
to set up an idol that will not fall over.

²¹ Do you not know?
Have you not heard?
Has it not been declared to you
from the beginning?
Have you not considered
the foundations of the earth?
²² God is enthroned above the circle of
  the earth;
its inhabitants are like grasshoppers.
He stretches out the heavens like thin cloth
and spreads them out like a tent to live in.
²³ He reduces princes to nothing
and makes judges of the earth like
  a wasteland.
²⁴ They are barely planted, barely sown,
their stem hardly takes root in the ground
when he blows on them and they wither,
and a whirlwind carries them away
  like stubble.

²⁵ "To whom will you compare me,
or who is my equal?" asks the Holy One.
²⁶ Look up and see!
Who created these?
He brings out the stars by number;
he calls all of them by name.
Because of his great power and strength,
not one of them is missing.

²⁷ Jacob, why do you say,
and Israel, why do you assert,
"My way is hidden from the Lord,
and my claim is ignored by my God"?
²⁸ Do you not know?
Have you not heard?
The Lord is the everlasting God,
the Creator of the whole earth.
He never becomes faint or weary;
there is no limit to his understanding.
²⁹ He gives strength to the faint
and strengthens the powerless.
³⁰ Youths may become faint and weary,
and young men stumble and fall,
³¹ but those who trust in the Lord
will renew their strength;
they will soar on wings like eagles;
they will run and not become weary,
they will walk and not faint.

ISAIAH 41

THE LORD VERSUS THE NATIONS' GODS

¹ "Be silent before me, coasts and islands!
And let peoples renew their strength.
Let them approach; let them testify;
let's come together for the trial.
² Who has stirred up someone from the east?
In righteousness he calls him to serve.
The Lord hands nations over to him,
and he subdues kings.
He makes them like dust with his sword,
like wind-driven stubble with his bow.
³ He pursues them, going on safely,
hardly touching the path with his feet.
⁴ Who has performed and done this,
calling the generations from the beginning?

I am the Lord, the first
and with the last—I am he."

⁵ The coasts and islands see and are afraid,
the whole earth trembles.
They approach and arrive.
⁶ Each one helps the other,
and says to another, "Take courage!"
⁷ The craftsman encourages the metalworker;
the one who flattens with the hammer
encourages the one who strikes the anvil,
saying of the soldering, "It is good."
He fastens it with nails so that it will not fall over.

⁸ But you, Israel, my servant,
Jacob, whom I have chosen,
descendant of Abraham, my friend—
⁹ I brought you from the ends of the earth
and called you from its farthest corners.
I said to you: You are my servant;
I have chosen you; I haven't rejected you.
¹⁰ Do not fear, for I am with you;
do not be afraid, for I am your God.
I will strengthen you; I will help you;
I will hold on to you with my righteous right hand.

¹¹ Be sure that all who are enraged against you
will be ashamed and disgraced;
those who contend with you
will become as nothing and will perish.
¹² You will look for those who contend with you,
but you will not find them.
Those who war against you
will become absolutely nothing.
¹³ For I am the Lord your God,
who holds your right hand,
who says to you, "Do not fear,
I will help you.
¹⁴ Do not fear, you worm Jacob,
you men of Israel.
I will help you"—
    this is the Lord's declaration.

NOTES

Your Redeemer is the Holy One of Israel.
¹⁵ See, I will make you into a sharp threshing board,
new, with many teeth.
You will thresh mountains and pulverize them
and make hills into chaff.
¹⁶ You will winnow them
and a wind will carry them away,
a whirlwind will scatter them.
But you will rejoice in the Lord;
you will boast in the Holy One of Israel.

¹⁷ The poor and the needy seek water, but there is none;
their tongues are parched with thirst.
I will answer them.
I am the Lord, the God of Israel. I will not abandon them.
¹⁸ I will open rivers on the barren heights,
and springs in the middle of the plains.
I will turn the desert into a pool
and dry land into springs.
¹⁹ I will plant cedar, acacia, myrtle, and olive trees
in the wilderness.
I will put juniper, elm, and cypress trees together
in the desert,
²⁰ so that all may see and know,
consider and understand,
that the hand of the Lord has done this,
the Holy One of Israel has created it.

²¹ "Submit your case," says the Lord.
"Present your arguments," says Jacob's King.
²² "Let them come and tell us
what will happen.
Tell us the past events,
so that we may reflect on them
and know the outcome,
or tell us the future.
²³ Tell us the coming events,
then we will know that you are gods.
Indeed, do something good or bad,
then we will be in awe when we see it.

NOTES

²⁴ Look, you are nothing
and your work is worthless.
Anyone who chooses you is detestable.

²⁵ "I have stirred up one from the north, and he has come,
one from the east who invokes my name.
He will march over rulers as if they were mud,
like a potter who treads the clay.
²⁶ Who told about this from the beginning,
so that we might know,
and from times past,
so that we might say, 'He is right'?
No one announced it,
no one told it,
no one heard your words.
²⁷ I was the first to say to Zion,
'Look! Here they are!'
And I gave Jerusalem a herald with good news.
²⁸ When I look, there is no one;
there is no counselor among them;
when I ask them, they have nothing to say.
²⁹ Look, all of them are a delusion;
their works are nonexistent;
their images are wind and emptiness."

GOING DEEPER

2 CORINTHIANS 1:3–7

THE GOD OF COMFORT

³ Blessed be the God and Father of our Lord Jesus Christ, the Father of mercies and the God of all comfort. ⁴ He comforts us in all our affliction, so that we may be able to comfort those who are in any kind of affliction, through the comfort we ourselves receive from God. ⁵ For just as the sufferings of Christ overflow to us, so also through Christ our comfort overflows. ⁶ If we are afflicted, it is for your comfort and salvation. If we are comforted, it is for your comfort, which produces in you patient endurance of the same sufferings that we suffer. ⁷ And our hope for you is firm, because we know that as you share in the sufferings, so you will also share in the comfort.

THE SERVANT'S MISSION

DAY 26   SECTION 2

Isaiah 42:1-4 is the first of four portions of Isaiah that many scholars highlight as the Servant Songs. These passages refer specifically to the "servant of the Lord," an individual who would serve God in all the ways that Israel fell short. Many New Testament writers point to these texts as referring to Jesus. As you continue reading, look for the other three Servant Songs:

- *Isaiah 49:1-6*
- *Isaiah 50:4-9*
- *Isaiah 52:13-53:12*

For more insight into the ways many of the prophecies that appear in Isaiah were ultimately fulfilled in Jesus, turn to page 214.

ISAIAH 42

THE SERVANT'S MISSION

¹ "This is my servant; I strengthen him,
this is my chosen one; I delight in him.
I have put my Spirit on him;
he will bring justice to the nations.
² He will not cry out or shout
or make his voice heard in the streets.
³ He will not break a bruised reed,
and he will not put out a smoldering wick;
he will faithfully bring justice.
⁴ He will not grow weak or be discouraged
until he has established justice on earth.
The coasts and islands will wait for his instruction."

⁵ This is what God, the Lord, says—
who created the heavens and stretched them out,
who spread out the earth and what comes from it,
who gives breath to the people on it
and spirit to those who walk on it—
⁶ "I am the Lord. I have called you
for a righteous purpose,
and I will hold you by your hand.
I will watch over you, and I will appoint you
to be a covenant for the people
and a light to the nations,
⁷ in order to open blind eyes,
to bring out prisoners from the dungeon,
and those sitting in darkness from the prison house.

⁸ I am the Lord. That is my name,
and I will not give my glory to another
or my praise to idols.
⁹ The past events have indeed happened.
Now I declare new events;
I announce them to you before they occur."

A SONG OF PRAISE

¹⁰ Sing a new song to the Lord;
sing his praise from the ends of the earth,
you who go down to the sea with all that
    fills it,
you coasts and islands with your inhabitants.
¹¹ Let the desert and its cities shout,
the settlements where Kedar dwells cry aloud.
Let the inhabitants of Sela sing for joy;
let them cry out from the mountaintops.
¹² Let them give glory to the Lord
and declare his praise in the coasts
    and islands.
¹³ The Lord advances like a warrior;
he stirs up his zeal like a soldier.
He shouts, he roars aloud,
he prevails over his enemies.

¹⁴ "I have kept silent from ages past;
I have been quiet and restrained myself.
But now, I will groan like a woman in labor,
gasping breathlessly.
¹⁵ I will lay waste mountains and hills
and dry up all their vegetation.
I will turn rivers into islands
and dry up marshes.
¹⁶ I will lead the blind by a way they did
    not know;
I will guide them on paths they have
    not known.
I will turn darkness to light in front of them
and rough places into level ground.
This is what I will do for them,
and I will not abandon them.

¹⁷ They will be turned back and
    utterly ashamed—
those who trust in an idol
and say to a cast image,
'You are our gods!'

ISRAEL'S BLINDNESS AND DEAFNESS

¹⁸ "Listen, you deaf!
Look, you blind, so that you may see.
¹⁹ Who is blind but my servant,
or deaf like my messenger I am sending?
Who is blind like my dedicated one,
or blind like the servant of the Lord?
²⁰ Though seeing many things, you pay
    no attention.
Though his ears are open, he does
    not listen."

²¹ Because of his righteousness, the Lord
    was pleased
to magnify his instruction and make
    it glorious.
²² But this is a people plundered and looted,
all of them trapped in holes
or imprisoned in dungeons.
They have become plunder
with no one to rescue them
and loot, with no one saying, "Give it back!"
²³ Who among you will hear this?
Let him listen and obey in the future.
²⁴ Who gave Jacob to the robber,
and Israel to the plunderers?
Was it not the Lord?
Have we not sinned against him?
They were not willing to walk in his ways,
and they would not listen to his instruction.
²⁵ So he poured out his furious anger
and the power of war on Jacob.
It surrounded him with fire, but he did not
    know it;
it burned him, but he didn't take it to heart.

ISAIAH 43

RESTORATION OF ISRAEL

¹ Now this is what the Lord says—
the one who created you, Jacob,
and the one who formed you, Israel—
"Do not fear, for I have redeemed you;
I have called you by your name; you are mine.
² When you pass through the waters,
I will be with you,
and the rivers will not overwhelm you.
When you walk through the fire,
you will not be scorched,
and the flame will not burn you.
³ For I am the Lord your God,
the Holy One of Israel, and your Savior.
I have given Egypt as a ransom for you,
Cush and Seba in your place.
⁴ Because you are precious in my sight
and honored, and I love you,
I will give people in exchange for you
and nations instead of your life.
⁵ Do not fear, for I am with you;
I will bring your descendants from the east,
and gather you from the west.
⁶ I will say to the north, 'Give them up!'
and to the south, 'Do not hold them back!'
Bring my sons from far away,
and my daughters from the ends of
 the earth—
⁷ everyone who bears my name
and is created for my glory.
I have formed them; indeed, I have
 made them."

⁸ Bring out a people who are blind, yet
 have eyes,
and are deaf, yet have ears.
⁹ All the nations are gathered together,
and the peoples are assembled.
Who among them can declare this,
and tell us the former things?

Let them present their witnesses
to vindicate themselves,
so that people may hear and say, "It is true."
¹⁰ "You are my witnesses"—
 this is the Lord's declaration—
"and my servant whom I have chosen,
so that you may know and believe me
and understand that I am he.
No god was formed before me,
and there will be none after me.
¹¹ I—I am the Lord.
Besides me, there is no Savior.
¹² I alone declared, saved, and proclaimed—
and not some foreign god among you.
So you are my witnesses"—
 this is the Lord's declaration—
"and I am God.
¹³ Also, from today on I am he alone,
and none can rescue from my power.
I act, and who can reverse it?"

GOD'S DELIVERANCE OF REBELLIOUS ISRAEL

¹⁴ This is what the Lord, your Redeemer, the Holy One of Israel says:

Because of you, I will send an army to Babylon
and bring all of them as fugitives,
even the Chaldeans in the ships in which
 they rejoice.
¹⁵ I am the Lord, your Holy One,
the Creator of Israel, your King.

¹⁶ This is what the Lord says—
who makes a way in the sea,
and a path through raging water,
¹⁷ who brings out the chariot and horse,
the army and the mighty one together
(they lie down, they do not rise again;
they are extinguished, put out like a wick)—
¹⁸ "Do not remember the past events;

pay no attention to things of old.
¹⁹ Look, I am about to do something new;
even now it is coming. Do you not see it?
Indeed, I will make a way in the wilderness,
rivers in the desert.
²⁰ Wild animals—
jackals and ostriches—will honor me,
because I provide water in the wilderness,
and rivers in the desert,
to give drink to my chosen people.
²¹ The people I formed for myself
will declare my praise.

²² "But, Jacob, you have not called on me,
because, Israel, you have become weary of me.
²³ You have not brought me your sheep for burnt offerings
or honored me with your sacrifices.
I have not burdened you with offerings
or wearied you with incense.
²⁴ You have not bought me aromatic cane with silver,
or satisfied me with the fat of your sacrifices.
But you have burdened me with your sins;
you have wearied me with your iniquities.

²⁵ "I am the one, I sweep away your transgressions
for my own sake
and remember your sins no more.
²⁶ Remind me. Let's argue the case together.
Recount the facts, so that you may be vindicated.
²⁷ Your first father sinned,
and your mediators have rebelled against me.
²⁸ So I defiled the officers of the sanctuary,
and set Jacob apart for destruction
and Israel for scorn."

ISAIAH 44:1–23

SPIRITUAL BLESSING

¹ "And now listen, Jacob my servant,
Israel whom I have chosen.
² This is the word of the Lord

your Maker, the one who formed you from
    the womb:
He will help you.
Do not fear, Jacob my servant,
Jeshurun whom I have chosen.
³ For I will pour water on the thirsty land
and streams on the dry ground;
I will pour out my Spirit on your descendants
and my blessing on your offspring.
⁴ They will sprout among the grass
like poplars by flowing streams.
⁵ This one will say, 'I am the Lord's';
another will use the name of Jacob;
still another will write on his hand,
    'The Lord's,'
and take on the name of Israel."

NO GOD OTHER THAN THE LORD

⁶ This is what the Lord, the King of Israel and its Redeemer, the Lord of Armies, says:

I am the first and I am the last.
There is no God but me.
⁷ Who, like me, can announce the future?
Let him say so and make a case before me,
since I have established an ancient people.
Let these gods declare the coming things,
and what will take place.
⁸ Do not be startled or afraid.
Have I not told you and declared it long ago?
You are my witnesses!
Is there any God but me?
There is no other Rock; I do not know any.

⁹ All who make idols are nothing,
and what they treasure benefits no one.
Their witnesses do not see or know anything,
so they will be put to shame.
¹⁰ Who makes a god or casts a metal image
that benefits no one?
¹¹ Look, all its worshipers will be put to shame,
and the craftsmen are humans.
They all will assemble and stand;
they all will be startled and put to shame.

¹² The ironworker labors over the coals,
shapes the idol with hammers,
and works it with his strong arm.
Also he grows hungry and his strength fails;
he doesn't drink water and is faint.
¹³ The woodworker stretches out a
    measuring line,
he outlines it with a stylus;
he shapes it with chisels
and outlines it with a compass.
He makes it according to a human form,
like a beautiful person,
to dwell in a temple.
¹⁴ He cuts down cedars for his use,
or he takes a cypress or an oak.
He lets it grow strong among the trees of
    the forest.
He plants a laurel, and the rain makes it grow.
¹⁵ A person can use it for fuel.
He takes some of it and warms himself;
also he kindles a fire and bakes bread;
he even makes it into a god and worships it;
he makes an idol from it and bows down to it.
¹⁶ He burns half of it in a fire,
and he roasts meat on that half.
He eats the roast and is satisfied.
He warms himself and says, "Ah!
I am warm, I see the blaze."
¹⁷ He makes a god or his idol with the rest
    of it.
He bows down to it and worships;
he prays to it, "Save me, for you are my god."
¹⁸ Such people do not comprehend
and cannot understand,
for he has shut their eyes so they cannot see,

and their minds so they cannot understand.
¹⁹ No one comes to his senses;
no one has the perception or insight to say,
"I burned half of it in the fire,
I also baked bread on its coals,
I roasted meat and ate.
Should I make something detestable with the rest of it?
Should I bow down to a block of wood?"
²⁰ He feeds on ashes.
His deceived mind has led him astray,
and he cannot rescue himself,
or say, "Isn't there a lie in my right hand?"

²¹ Remember these things, Jacob,
and Israel, for you are my servant;
I formed you, you are my servant;
Israel, you will never be forgotten by me.
²² I have swept away your transgressions like a cloud,
and your sins like a mist.
Return to me,
for I have redeemed you.
²³ Rejoice, heavens, for the LORD has acted;
shout, depths of the earth.
Break out into singing, mountains,
forest, and every tree in it.
For the LORD has redeemed Jacob,
and glorifies himself through Israel.

GOING DEEPER

MATTHEW 20:25-28

²⁵ Jesus called them over and said, "You know that the rulers of the Gentiles lord it over them, and those in high positions act as tyrants over them. ²⁶ It must not be like that among you. On the contrary, whoever wants to become great among you must be your servant, ²⁷ and whoever wants to be first among you must be your slave; ²⁸ just as the Son of Man did not come to be served, but to serve, and to give his life as a ransom for many."

WEEK FOUR
RESPONSE

USE THE FOLLOWING WORKSHEET TO HELP YOU REFLECT ON THIS WEEK'S READING.

Places or people the prophecies in this week's reading were directed toward:

An encouraging or challenging verse:

Isaiah :

A question to ponder and investigate:

Descriptive details about God and His people:

God

His People

How God's people were called to respond:

Specific sins revealed or warnings given:

GOD'S HOLINESS	How was God's holiness demonstrated in this week's reading? Circle one expression of His holiness in your answer above that stands out to you. How might trusting in this aspect of God strengthen your faith this Lenten season?
THE PEOPLE'S SIN	Review the sins that you listed on the previous page and consider how some of them may be present in your own life, even if they are expressed in different ways. Circle one that stands out to you and then use this space to reflect on the ways this sin appears in your own life.
HOPE FOR SALVATION THROUGH GOD	God responds to His people's sin and rebellion with a promise to save and restore them. Looking back on this week's reading, highlight or underline some of God's promises to His people. Having reflected on God's holiness and the reality of sin, how do these messages of hope encourage you as you journey through this season of Lent?

DAY 27

GRACE DAY

SECTION 2

Take this day to catch up on your reading, pray, and rest in the presence of the Lord.

THE LORD YOUR GOD IS AMONG YOU, A WARRIOR WHO SAVES. HE WILL REJOICE OVER YOU WITH GLADNESS. HE WILL BE QUIET IN HIS LOVE. HE WILL DELIGHT IN YOU WITH SINGING.

ZEPHANIAH 3:17

WEEKLY

DAY _____

Scripture is God breathed and true. When we memorize it, we carry His Word with us wherever we go.

During this reading plan, we are memorizing our key verse, Isaiah 43:1. This week, we'll continue with the final line of the verse.

SEE TIPS FOR MEMORIZING SCRIPTURE ON PAGE 272.

28 TRUTH

ISAIAH 43:1

Now this is what the LORD says—the one who created you, Jacob, and the one who formed you, Israel—"Do not fear, for I have redeemed you; I have called you by your name; you are mine."

DAY 29 　　　　　　　　　　　　　SECTION 2

GOD ALONE IS THE SAVIOR

ISAIAH 44:24–28

RESTORATION OF ISRAEL THROUGH CYRUS

²⁴ This is what the LORD, your Redeemer who formed you from the womb, says:

I am the LORD, who made everything;
who stretched out the heavens by myself;
who alone spread out the earth;
²⁵ who destroys the omens of the false prophets
and makes fools of diviners;
who confounds the wise
and makes their knowledge foolishness;
²⁶ who confirms the message of his servant
and fulfills the counsel of his messengers;
who says to Jerusalem, "She will be inhabited,"
and to the cities of Judah, "They will be rebuilt,"
and I will restore her ruins;
²⁷ who says to the depths of the sea, "Be dry,"
and I will dry up your rivers;
²⁸ who says to Cyrus, "My shepherd,
he will fulfill all my pleasure"
and says to Jerusalem, "She will be rebuilt,"
and of the temple, "Its foundation will be laid."

ISAIAH 45

¹ The Lord says this to Cyrus, his anointed,
whose right hand I have grasped
to subdue nations before him
and disarm kings,
to open doors before him,
and even city gates will not be shut:
² "I will go before you
and level the uneven places;
I will shatter the bronze doors
and cut the iron bars in two.
³ I will give you the treasures of darkness
and riches from secret places,
so that you may know that I am the Lord.
I am the God of Israel, who calls you by your name.
⁴ I call you by your name,
for the sake of my servant Jacob
and Israel my chosen one.
I give a name to you,
though you do not know me.
⁵ I am the Lord, and there is no other;
there is no God but me.
I will strengthen you,
though you do not know me,
⁶ so that all may know from the rising of the sun to its setting
that there is no one but me.
I am the Lord, and there is no other.
⁷ I form light and create darkness,
I make success and create disaster;
I am the Lord, who does all these things.

⁸ "Heavens, sprinkle from above,
and let the skies shower righteousness.
Let the earth open up
so that salvation will sprout
and righteousness will spring up with it.
I, the Lord, have created it.

⁹ "Woe to the one who argues with his Maker—
one clay pot among many.
Does clay say to the one forming it,

NOTES

'What are you making?'
Or does your work say,
'He has no hands'?
¹⁰ Woe to the one who says to his father,
'What are you fathering?'
or to his mother,
'What are you giving birth to?'"
¹¹ This is what the Lord,
the Holy One of Israel and its Maker, says:
"Ask me what is to happen to my sons,
and instruct me about the work of my hands.
¹² I made the earth,
and created humans on it.
It was my hands that stretched out the heavens,
and I commanded everything in them.
¹³ I have stirred him up in righteousness,
and will level all roads for him.
He will rebuild my city,
and set my exiles free,
not for a price or a bribe,"
says the Lord of Armies.

GOD ALONE IS THE SAVIOR

¹⁴ This is what the Lord says:

"The products of Egypt and the merchandise of Cush
and the Sabeans, men of stature,
will come over to you
and will be yours;
they will follow you,
they will come over in chains
and bow down to you.
They will confess to you,
'God is indeed with you, and there is no other;
there is no other God.'"

¹⁵ Yes, you are a God who hides,
God of Israel, Savior.
¹⁶ All of them are put to shame, even humiliated;
the makers of idols go in humiliation together.
¹⁷ Israel will be saved by the Lord

with an everlasting salvation;
you will not be put to shame or humiliated
for all eternity.

¹⁸ For this is what the LORD says—
the Creator of the heavens,
the God who formed the earth and made it,
the one who established it
(he did not create it to be a wasteland,
but formed it to be inhabited)—
he says, "I am the LORD,
and there is no other.
¹⁹ I have not spoken in secret,
somewhere in a land of darkness.
I did not say to the descendants of Jacob:
Seek me in a wasteland.
I am the LORD, who speaks righteously,
who declares what is right.

²⁰ "Come, gather together,
and approach, you fugitives of the nations.
Those who carry their wooden idols
and pray to a god who cannot save
have no knowledge.
²¹ Speak up and present your case—
yes, let them consult each other.
Who predicted this long ago?
Who announced it from ancient times?
Was it not I, the LORD?
There is no other God but me,
a righteous God and Savior;
there is no one except me.
²² Turn to me and be saved,
all the ends of the earth.
For I am God,
and there is no other.
²³ By myself I have sworn;
truth has gone from my mouth,
a word that will not be revoked:
Every knee will bow to me,
every tongue will swear allegiance.

NOTES

NOTES

²⁴ It will be said about me, 'Righteousness and strength
are found only in the Lord.'"
All who are enraged against him
will come to him and be put to shame.
²⁵ All the descendants of Israel
will be justified and boast in the Lord.

ISAIAH 46

THERE IS NO ONE LIKE GOD

¹ Bel crouches; Nebo cowers.
Idols depicting them are consigned to beasts and cattle.
The images you carry are loaded,
as a burden for the weary animal.
² The gods cower; they crouch together;
they are not able to rescue the burden,
but they themselves go into captivity.

³ "Listen to me, house of Jacob,
all the remnant of the house of Israel,
who have been sustained from the womb,
carried along since birth.
⁴ I will be the same until your old age,
and I will bear you up when you turn gray.
I have made you, and I will carry you;
I will bear and rescue you.

⁵ "To whom will you compare me or make me equal?
Who will you measure me with,
so that we should be like each other?
⁶ Those who pour out their bags of gold
and weigh out silver on scales—
they hire a goldsmith and he makes it into a god.
Then they kneel and bow down to it.
⁷ They lift it to their shoulder and bear it along;
they set it in its place, and there it stands;
it does not budge from its place.
They cry out to it but it doesn't answer;
it saves no one from his trouble.

⁸ "Remember this and be brave;

take it to heart, you transgressors!

⁹ Remember what happened long ago,
for I am God, and there is no other;
I am God, and no one is like me.
¹⁰ I declare the end from the beginning,
and from long ago what is not yet done,
saying: my plan will take place,
and I will do all my will.
¹¹ I call a bird of prey from the east,
a man for my purpose from a far country.
Yes, I have spoken; so I will also bring it about.
I have planned it; I will also do it.
¹² Listen to me, you hardhearted,
far removed from justice:
¹³ I am bringing my justice near;
it is not far away,
and my salvation will not delay.
I will put salvation in Zion,
my splendor in Israel."

GOING DEEPER

1 PETER 1:3-5, 10-12

A LIVING HOPE

³ Blessed be the God and Father of our Lord Jesus Christ. Because of his great mercy he has given us new birth into a living hope through the resurrection of Jesus Christ from the dead ⁴ and into an inheritance that is imperishable, undefiled, and unfading, kept in heaven for you. ⁵ You are being guarded by God's power through faith for a salvation that is ready to be revealed in the last time.

…

¹⁰ Concerning this salvation, the prophets, who prophesied about the grace that would come to you, searched and carefully investigated. ¹¹ They inquired into what time or what circumstances the Spirit of Christ within them was indicating when he testified in advance to the sufferings of Christ and the glories that would follow. ¹² It was revealed to them that they were not serving themselves but you. These things have now been announced to you through those who preached the gospel to you by the Holy Spirit sent from heaven—angels long to catch a glimpse of these things.

NAMES FOR GOD IN ISAIAH

Branch of the Lord

GOD OF ISRAEL

Creator

Creator of Israel

Father

Eternal Father

High and Exalted One

God

Holy One of Jacob

Holy One

HOLY ONE OF ISRAEL

Israel's Light

Immanuel

Holy Spirit

King

Judge

Lawgiver

King of Israel

Lord

Lord

Lord God

Living God

Throughout the book of Isaiah, God is described through the use of many different names. Sometimes the names are formal names we see throughout Scripture, such as Lord. Other names function within the images and context of Isaiah, helping us to better understand God's nature, work, and relationship with His people. Here you will find a list of several of these names as they appear in the CSB translation, all to help shape our understanding of God's identity throughout this prophetic book. Take time to read each name one by one. As you engage with this list and continue reading Isaiah, this space is for you to mark or jot down notes around the ones that have been meaningful, hopeful, or encouraging to you during this Lenten season.

Lord our God

Lord God of Armies

Maker

LORD OF ARMIES

Lord your God

Rock

Most High

Mighty God

Mighty One of Israel

Lord, the God of Israel

REDEEMER

Mighty One of Jacob

Righteous One

Prince of Peace

Savior

Rock of Israel

Redeemer of Israel

Spirit

Spirit of the Lord

Teacher

Spirit of the Lord God

Wonderful Counselor

THE SERVANT BRINGS SALVATION

DAY 30   SECTION 2

ISAIAH 47

THE FALL OF BABYLON

¹ "Go down and sit in the dust,
Virgin Daughter Babylon.
Sit on the ground without a throne,
Daughter Chaldea!
For you will no longer be called pampered
    and spoiled.
² Take millstones and grind flour;
remove your veil,
strip off your skirt, bare your thigh,
wade through the streams.
³ Your nakedness will be uncovered,
and your disgrace will be exposed.
I will take vengeance;
I will spare no one."
⁴ The Holy One of Israel is our Redeemer;
The Lord of Armies is his name.

⁵ "Daughter Chaldea,
sit in silence and go into darkness.
For you will no longer be called mistress
    of kingdoms.
⁶ I was angry with my people;
I profaned my possession,
and I handed them over to you.
You showed them no mercy;
you made your yoke very heavy on
    the elderly.
⁷ You said, 'I will be the queen forever.'
You did not take these things to heart
or think about their outcome.

⁸ "So now hear this, lover of luxury,
who sits securely,
who says to herself,
'I am, and there is no one else.
I will never be a widow
or know the loss of children.'
⁹ These two things will happen to you
suddenly, in one day:
loss of children and widowhood.
They will happen to you in their entirety,
in spite of your many sorceries
and the potency of your spells.
¹⁰ You were secure in your wickedness;
you said, 'No one sees me.'
Your wisdom and knowledge
led you astray.
You said to yourself,
'I am, and there is no one else.'
¹¹ But disaster will happen to you;

you will not know how to avert it.
And it will fall on you,
but you will be unable to ward it off.
Devastation will happen to you suddenly
and unexpectedly.

¹² So take your stand with your spells
and your many sorceries,
which you have wearied yourself with from
   your youth.
Perhaps you will be able to succeed;
perhaps you will inspire terror!
¹³ You are worn out with your
   many consultations.
So let the astrologers stand and save you—
those who observe the stars,
those who predict monthly
what will happen to you.
¹⁴ Look, they are like stubble;
fire burns them.
They cannot rescue themselves
from the power of the flame.
This is not a coal for warming themselves,
or a fire to sit beside!
¹⁵ This is what they are to you—
those who have wearied you
and have traded with you from your youth—
each wanders on his own way;
no one can save you."

ISAIAH 48

ISRAEL MUST LEAVE BABYLON

¹ "Listen to this, house of Jacob—
those who are called by the name Israel
and have descended from Judah,
who swear by the name of the LORD
and declare the God of Israel,
but not in truth or righteousness.
² For they are named after the holy city,
and lean on the God of Israel;
his name is the LORD of Armies.
³ I declared the past events long ago;
they came out of my mouth; I
   proclaimed them.
Suddenly I acted, and they occurred.
⁴ Because I know that you are stubborn,
and your neck is iron
and your forehead bronze,
⁵ therefore I declared to you long ago.
I announced it to you before it occurred,
so you could not claim, 'My idol
   caused them;
my carved image and cast idol control them.'
⁶ You have heard it. Observe it all.
Will you not acknowledge it?
From now on I will announce new things
   to you,
hidden things that you have not known.
⁷ They have been created now, and not
   long ago;
you have not heard of them before today,
so you could not claim, 'I already
   knew them!'
⁸ You have never heard; you have
   never known;
for a long time your ears have not been open.
For I knew that you were very treacherous,
and were known as a rebel from birth.
⁹ I will delay my anger for the sake of
   my name,
and I will restrain myself for your benefit and
   for my praise,
so that you will not be destroyed.
¹⁰ Look, I have refined you, but not as silver;
I have tested you in the furnace of affliction.
¹¹ I will act for my own sake, indeed, my own,
for how can I be defiled?
I will not give my glory to another.
¹² "Listen to me, Jacob,
and Israel, the one called by me:
I am he; I am the first,

I am also the last.
¹³ My own hand founded the earth,
and my right hand spread out the heavens;
when I summoned them,
they stood up together.
¹⁴ All of you, assemble and listen!
Who among the idols has declared
    these things?
The Lord loves him;
he will accomplish his will against Babylon,
and his arm will be against the Chaldeans.
¹⁵ I—I have spoken;
yes, I have called him;
I have brought him,
and he will succeed in his mission.
¹⁶ Approach me and listen to this.
From the beginning I have not spoken
    in secret;
from the time anything existed, I was there."
And now the Lord God
has sent me and his Spirit.

¹⁷ This is what the Lord, your Redeemer, the Holy One of Israel says:

I am the Lord your God,
who teaches you for your benefit,
who leads you in the way you should go.
¹⁸ If only you had paid attention to
    my commands.
Then your peace would have been like a river,
and your righteousness like the waves of
    the sea.
¹⁹ Your descendants would have been as
    countless as the sand,
and the offspring of your body like its grains;
their name would not be cut off
or eliminated from my presence.

²⁰ Leave Babylon,
    flee from the Chaldeans!
Declare with a shout of joy,
proclaim this,
let it go out to the end of the earth;
announce,
"The Lord has redeemed his servant Jacob!"
²¹ They did not thirst
when he led them through the deserts;
he made water flow from the rock for them;
he split the rock, and water gushed out.
²² "There is no peace for the wicked," says
    the Lord.

ISAIAH 49

THE SERVANT BRINGS SALVATION

¹ Coasts and islands, listen to me;
distant peoples, pay attention.
The Lord called me before I was born.
He named me while I was in my
    mother's womb.
² He made my words like a sharp sword;
he hid me in the shadow of his hand.
He made me like a sharpened arrow;
he hid me in his quiver.
³ He said to me, "You are my servant,
Israel, in whom I will be glorified."
⁴ But I myself said: I have labored in vain,
I have spent my strength for nothing
    and futility;
yet my vindication is with the Lord,
and my reward is with my God.
⁵ And now, says the Lord,
who formed me from the womb to be
    his servant,
to bring Jacob back to him
so that Israel might be gathered to him;
for I am honored in the sight of the Lord,
and my God is my strength—
⁶ he says,
"It is not enough for you to be my servant

raising up the tribes of Jacob
and restoring the protected ones of Israel.
I will also make you a light for the nations,
to be my salvation to the ends of the earth."
⁷ This is what the LORD,
the Redeemer of Israel, his Holy One, says
to one who is despised,
to one abhorred by people,
to a servant of rulers:
"Kings will see, princes will stand up,
and they will all bow down
because of the LORD, who is faithful,
the Holy One of Israel—and he has chosen you."

⁸ This is what the LORD says:

I will answer you in a time of favor,
and I will help you in the day of salvation.
I will keep you, and I will appoint you
to be a covenant for the people,
to restore the land,
to make them possess the desolate inheritances,
⁹ saying to the prisoners, "Come out,"
and to those who are in darkness, "Show yourselves."
They will feed along the pathways,
and their pastures will be on all the barren heights.
¹⁰ They will not hunger or thirst,
the scorching heat or sun will not strike them;
for their compassionate one will guide them,
and lead them to springs.
¹¹ I will make all my mountains into a road,
and my highways will be raised up.
¹² See, these will come from far away,
from the north and from the west,
and from the land of Sinim.

¹³ Shout for joy, you heavens!
Earth, rejoice!
Mountains break into joyful shouts!
For the LORD has comforted his people,
and will have compassion on his afflicted ones.

NOTES

¹⁴ Zion says, "The Lord has abandoned me;
the Lord has forgotten me!"
¹⁵ "Can a woman forget her nursing child,
or lack compassion for the child of
    her womb?
Even if these forget,
yet I will not forget you.
¹⁶ Look, I have inscribed you on the palms
    of my hands;
your walls are continually before me.
¹⁷ Your builders hurry;
those who destroy and devastate you will
    leave you.
¹⁸ Look up, and look around.
They all gather together; they come to you.
As I live"—
    this is the Lord's declaration—
"you will wear all your children as jewelry,
and put them on as a bride does.
¹⁹ For your waste and desolate places
and your land marked by ruins
will now be indeed too small for
    the inhabitants,
and those who swallowed you up will be
    far away.
²⁰ Yet as you listen, the children
that you have been deprived of will say,
'This place is too small for me;
make room for me so that I may settle.'
²¹ Then you will say within yourself,
'Who fathered these for me?
I was deprived of my children and unable
    to conceive,
exiled and wandering—
but who brought them up?
See, I was left by myself—
but these, where did they come from?'"

²² This is what the Lord God says:

Look, I will lift up my hand to the nations,
and raise my banner to the peoples.
They will bring your sons in their arms,
and your daughters will be carried on
    their shoulders.
²³ Kings will be your guardians
and their queens your nursing mothers.
They will bow down to you
with their faces to the ground
and lick the dust at your feet.
Then you will know that I am the Lord;
those who put their hope in me
will not be put to shame.

²⁴ Can the prey be taken from a mighty man,
or the captives of a tyrant be delivered?
²⁵ For this is what the Lord says:
"Even the captives of a mighty man will
    be taken,
and the prey of a tyrant will be delivered;
I will contend with the one who contends
    with you,
and I will save your children.
²⁶ I will make your oppressors eat their
    own flesh,
and they will be drunk with their own blood
as with sweet wine.
Then all humanity will know
that I, the Lord, am your Savior,
and your Redeemer, the Mighty One
    of Jacob."

ISAIAH 50:1-3

¹ This is what the Lord says:

Where is your mother's divorce certificate
that I used to send her away?
Or to which of my creditors did I sell you?

NOTES

Look, you were sold for your iniquities,
and your mother was sent away
because of your transgressions.
² Why was no one there when I came?
Why was there no one to answer when I called?
Is my arm too weak to redeem?
Or do I have no power to rescue?
Look, I dry up the sea by my rebuke;
I turn the rivers into a wilderness;
their fish rot because of lack of water
and die of thirst.
³ I dress the heavens in black
and make sackcloth their covering.

◼ GOING DEEPER

PSALM 23

THE GOOD SHEPHERD

A psalm of David.

¹ The Lord is my shepherd;
I have what I need.
² He lets me lie down in green pastures;
he leads me beside quiet waters.
³ He renews my life;
he leads me along the right paths
for his name's sake.
⁴ Even when I go through the darkest valley,
I fear no danger,
for you are with me;
your rod and your staff—they comfort me.

⁵ You prepare a table before me
in the presence of my enemies;
you anoint my head with oil;
my cup overflows.
⁶ Only goodness and faithful love will pursue me
all the days of my life,
and I will dwell in the house of the Lord
as long as I live.

DAY 31

SALVATION FOR ZION

SECTION 2

ISAIAH 50:4-11

THE OBEDIENT SERVANT

⁴ The Lord God has given me
the tongue of those who are instructed
to know how to sustain the weary with a word.
He awakens me each morning;
he awakens my ear to listen like those being instructed.
⁵ The Lord God has opened my ear,
and I was not rebellious;
I did not turn back.
⁶ I gave my back to those who beat me,
and my cheeks to those who tore out my beard.
I did not hide my face from scorn and spitting.

⁷ The Lord God will help me;
therefore I have not been humiliated;
therefore I have set my face like flint,
and I know I will not be put to shame.
⁸ The one who vindicates me is near;
who will contend with me?
Let us confront each other.
Who has a case against me?
Let him come near me!

⁹ In truth, the Lord God will help me;
who will condemn me?
Indeed, all of them will wear out like a garment;
a moth will devour them.
¹⁰ Who among you fears the Lord
and listens to his servant?
Who among you walks in darkness,
and has no light?
Let him trust in the name of the Lord;
let him lean on his God.
¹¹ Look, all you who kindle a fire,
who encircle yourselves with torches;
walk in the light of your fire
and of the torches you have lit!
This is what you'll get from my hand:
you will lie down in a place of torment.

ISAIAH 51

SALVATION FOR ZION

¹ Listen to me, you who pursue righteousness,
you who seek the LORD:
Look to the rock from which you were cut,
and to the quarry from which you were dug.
² Look to Abraham your father,
and to Sarah who gave birth to you.
When I called him, he was only one;
I blessed him and made him many.
³ For the LORD will comfort Zion;
he will comfort all her waste places,
and he will make her wilderness like Eden,
and her desert like the garden of the LORD.
Joy and gladness will be found in her,
thanksgiving and melodious song.
⁴ Pay attention to me, my people,
and listen to me, my nation;
for instruction will come from me,
and my justice for a light to the nations.
I will bring it about quickly.
⁵ My righteousness is near,
my salvation appears,
and my arms will bring justice to the nations.
The coasts and islands will put their hope
    in me,
and they will look to my strength.
⁶ Look up to the heavens,
and look at the earth beneath;
for the heavens will vanish like smoke,
the earth will wear out like a garment,
and its inhabitants will die like gnats.
But my salvation will last forever,
and my righteousness will never be shattered.
⁷ Listen to me, you who know righteousness,
the people in whose heart is my instruction:
do not fear disgrace by men,
and do not be shattered by their taunts.
⁸ For moths will devour them like a garment,
and worms will eat them like wool.
But my righteousness will last forever,
and my salvation for all generations.
⁹ Wake up, wake up!
Arm of the LORD, clothe yourself
    with strength.
Wake up as in days past,
as in generations long ago.
Wasn't it you who hacked Rahab to pieces,
who pierced the sea monster?
¹⁰ Wasn't it you who dried up the sea,
the waters of the great deep,
who made the sea-bed into a road
for the redeemed to pass over?
¹¹ And the ransomed of the LORD will return
and come to Zion with singing,
crowned with unending joy.
Joy and gladness will overtake them,
and sorrow and sighing will flee.

¹² I—I am the one who comforts you.
Who are you that you should fear humans
    who die,
or a son of man who is given up like grass?
¹³ But you have forgotten the LORD,
    your Maker,
who stretched out the heavens
and laid the foundations of the earth.
You are in constant dread all day long
because of the fury of the oppressor,
who has set himself to destroy.
But where is the fury of the oppressor?
¹⁴ The prisoner is soon to be set free;
he will not die and go to the Pit,
and his food will not be lacking.
¹⁵ For I am the LORD your God
who stirs up the sea so that its waves roar—
his name is the LORD of Armies.
¹⁶ I have put my words in your mouth,

and covered you in the shadow of my hand,
in order to plant the heavens,
to found the earth,
and to say to Zion, "You are my people."

¹⁷ Wake yourself, wake yourself up!
Stand up, Jerusalem,
you who have drunk the cup of his fury
from the Lord's hand;
you who have drunk the goblet to the dregs—
the cup that causes people to stagger.
¹⁸ There is no one to guide her
among all the children she has raised;
there is no one to take hold of her hand
among all the offspring she has brought up.
¹⁹ These two things have happened to you:
devastation and destruction,
famine and sword.
Who will grieve for you?
How can I comfort you?
²⁰ Your children have fainted;
they lie at the head of every street
like an antelope in a net.
They are full of the Lord's fury,
the rebuke of your God.

²¹ So listen to this, suffering
and drunken one—but not with wine.
²² This is what your Lord says—
the Lord, even your God,
who defends his people—
"Look, I have removed from your hand
the cup that causes staggering;
that goblet, the cup of my fury.
You will never drink it again.
²³ I will put it into the hands of your tormentors,
who said to you,
'Lie down, so we can walk over you.'
You made your back like the ground,
and like a street for those who walk on it."

NOTES

NOTES

ISAIAH 52:1-6

¹ "Wake up, wake up;
put on your strength, Zion!
Put on your beautiful garments,
Jerusalem, the holy city!
For the uncircumcised and the unclean
will no longer enter you.
² Stand up, shake the dust off yourself!
Take your seat, Jerusalem.
Remove the bonds from your neck,
captive Daughter Zion."
³ For this is what the LORD says:
"You were sold for nothing,
and you will be redeemed without silver."
⁴ For this is what the Lord GOD says:
"At first my people went down to Egypt to reside there,
then Assyria oppressed them without cause.
⁵ So now what have I here"—
    this is the LORD's declaration—
"that my people are taken away for nothing?
Its rulers wail"—
    this is the LORD's declaration—
"and my name is continually blasphemed all day long.
⁶ Therefore my people will know my name;
therefore they will know on that day
that I am he who says,
'Here I am.'"

◆ GOING DEEPER

DEUTERONOMY 30:19-20

¹⁹ I call heaven and earth as witnesses against you today that I have set before you life and death, blessing and curse. Choose life so that you and your descendants may live, ²⁰ love the LORD your God, obey him, and remain faithful to him. For he is your life, and he will prolong your days as you live in the land the LORD swore to give to your ancestors Abraham, Isaac, and Jacob.

1 JOHN 1:5–10

FELLOWSHIP WITH GOD

⁵ This is the message we have heard from him and declare to you: God is light, and there is absolutely no darkness in him. ⁶ If we say, "We have fellowship with him," and yet we walk in darkness, we are lying and are not practicing the truth. ⁷ If we walk in the light as he himself is in the light, we have fellowship with one another, and the blood of Jesus his Son cleanses us from all sin. ⁸ If we say, "We have no sin," we are deceiving ourselves, and the truth is not in us.

⁹ If we confess our sins, he is faithful and righteous to forgive us our sins and to cleanse us from all unrighteousness.

¹⁰ If we say, "We have not sinned," we make him a liar, and his word is not in us.

NOTES

THE SERVANT'S SUFFERING AND EXALTATION

YET THE LORD WAS PLEASED TO CRUSH HIM SEVERELY. WHEN YOU MAKE HIM A GUILT OFFERING, HE WILL SEE HIS SEED, HE WILL PROLONG HIS DAYS, AND BY HIS HAND, THE LORD'S PLEASURE WILL BE ACCOMPLISHED.

ISAIAH 53:10

DAY 32   SECTION 2

ISAIAH 52:7-15

⁷ How beautiful on the mountains
are the feet of the herald,
who proclaims peace,
who brings news of good things,
who proclaims salvation,
who says to Zion, "Your God reigns!"
⁸ The voices of your watchmen—
they lift up their voices,
shouting for joy together;
for every eye will see
when the Lord returns to Zion.
⁹ Be joyful, rejoice together,
you ruins of Jerusalem!
For the Lord has comforted his people;
he has redeemed Jerusalem.
¹⁰ The Lord has displayed his holy arm
in the sight of all the nations;
all the ends of the earth will see
the salvation of our God.

¹¹ Leave, leave, go out from there!
Do not touch anything unclean;
go out from her, purify yourselves,
you who carry the vessels of the Lord.
¹² For you will not leave in a hurry,
and you will not have to take flight;
because the Lord is going before you,
and the God of Israel is your rear guard.

THE SERVANT'S SUFFERING AND EXALTATION

¹³ See, my servant will be successful;
he will be raised and lifted up and
greatly exalted.

¹⁴ Just as many were appalled at you—
his appearance was so disfigured
that he did not look like a man,
and his form did not resemble a human being—
¹⁵ so he will sprinkle many nations.

Kings will shut their mouths because of him,
for they will see what had not been told them,
and they will understand what they had not heard.

ISAIAH 53

¹ Who has believed what we have heard?
And to whom has the arm of the Lord been revealed?
² He grew up before him like a young plant
and like a root out of dry ground.
He didn't have an impressive form
or majesty that we should look at him,
no appearance that we should desire him.
³ He was despised and rejected by men,
a man of suffering who knew what sickness was.
He was like someone people turned away from;
he was despised, and we didn't value him.

⁴ Yet he himself bore our sicknesses,
and he carried our pains;
but we in turn regarded him stricken,
struck down by God, and afflicted.
⁵ But he was pierced because of our rebellion,
crushed because of our iniquities;
punishment for our peace was on him,
and we are healed by his wounds.
⁶ We all went astray like sheep;
we all have turned to our own way;
and the Lord has punished him
for the iniquity of us all.

⁷ He was oppressed and afflicted,
yet he did not open his mouth.
Like a lamb led to the slaughter
and like a sheep silent before her shearers,
he did not open his mouth.
⁸ He was taken away because of oppression and judgment,
and who considered his fate?
For he was cut off from the land of the living;
he was struck because of my people's rebellion.

⁹ He was assigned a grave with the wicked,
but he was with a rich man at his death,
because he had done no violence
and had not spoken deceitfully.

¹⁰ Yet the Lord was pleased to crush him severely.
When you make him a guilt offering,
he will see his seed, he will prolong his days,
and by his hand, the Lord's pleasure will be accomplished.
¹¹ After his anguish,
he will see light and be satisfied.
By his knowledge,
my righteous servant will justify many,
and he will carry their iniquities.
¹² Therefore I will give him the many as a portion,
and he will receive the mighty as spoil,
because he willingly submitted to death,
and was counted among the rebels;
yet he bore the sin of many
and interceded for the rebels.

◗ GOING DEEPER

HEBREWS 2:9-10

⁹ But we do see Jesus—made lower than the angels for a short time so that by God's grace he might taste death for everyone—crowned with glory and honor because he suffered death.

¹⁰ For in bringing many sons and daughters to glory, it was entirely appropriate that God—for whom and through whom all things exist—should make the pioneer of their salvation perfect through sufferings.

1 PETER 2:24

He himself bore our sins in his body on the tree; so that, having died to sins, we might live for righteousness. By his wounds you have been healed.

HYMN

HALLELUJAH, WHAT A SAVIOR!

WORDS: PHILIP P. BLISS
MUSIC: PHILIP P. BLISS

COME TO THE LORD

DAY 33 — SECTION 2

ISAIAH 54

FUTURE GLORY FOR ISRAEL

¹ "Rejoice, childless one, who did not
 give birth;
burst into song and shout,
you who have not been in labor!
For the children of the desolate one will
 be more
than the children of the married woman,"
says the Lord.
² "Enlarge the site of your tent,
and let your tent curtains be stretched out;
do not hold back;
lengthen your ropes,
and drive your pegs deep.
³ For you will spread out to the right and to
 the left,
and your descendants will dispossess nations
and inhabit the desolate cities.

⁴ "Do not be afraid, for you will not be put
 to shame;
don't be humiliated, for you will not
 be disgraced.
For you will forget the shame of your youth,
and you will no longer remember
the disgrace of your widowhood.
⁵ Indeed, your husband is your Maker—
his name is the Lord of Armies—
and the Holy One of Israel is your Redeemer;
he is called the God of the whole earth.
⁶ For the Lord has called you,
like a wife deserted and wounded in spirit,
a wife of one's youth when she is rejected,"
says your God.
⁷ "I deserted you for a brief moment,
but I will take you back with
 abundant compassion.
⁸ In a surge of anger
I hid my face from you for a moment,
but I will have compassion on you
with everlasting love,"

NOTES

says the Lord your Redeemer.
⁹ "For this is like the days of Noah to me:
when I swore that the water of Noah
would never flood the earth again,
so I have sworn that I will not be angry with you
or rebuke you.
¹⁰ Though the mountains move
and the hills shake,
my love will not be removed from you
and my covenant of peace will not be shaken,"
says your compassionate Lord.

¹¹ "Poor Jerusalem, storm-tossed, and not comforted,
I will set your stones in black mortar,
and lay your foundations in lapis lazuli.
¹² I will make your fortifications out of rubies,
your gates out of sparkling stones,
and all your walls out of precious stones.
¹³ Then all your children will be taught by the Lord,
their prosperity will be great,
¹⁴ and you will be established
on a foundation of righteousness.
You will be far from oppression,
you will certainly not be afraid;
you will be far from terror,
it will certainly not come near you.
¹⁵ If anyone attacks you,
it is not from me;
whoever attacks you
will fall before you.
¹⁶ Look, I have created the craftsman
who blows on the charcoal fire
and produces a weapon suitable for its task;
and I have created the destroyer to cause havoc.
¹⁷ No weapon formed against you will succeed,
and you will refute any accusation
raised against you in court.
This is the heritage of the Lord's servants,
and their vindication is from me."

This is the Lord's declaration.

ISAIAH 55

COME TO THE LORD

¹ "Come, everyone who is thirsty,
come to the water;
and you without silver,
come, buy, and eat!
Come, buy wine and milk
without silver and without cost!
² Why do you spend silver on what is not food,
and your wages on what does not satisfy?
Listen carefully to me, and eat what is good,
and you will enjoy the choicest of foods.
³ Pay attention and come to me;
listen, so that you will live.
I will make a permanent covenant with you
on the basis of the faithful kindnesses of David.
⁴ Since I have made him a witness to the peoples,
a leader and commander for the peoples,
⁵ so you will summon a nation you do not know,
and nations who do not know you will run to you.
For the LORD your God,
even the Holy One of Israel,
has glorified you."

⁶ Seek the LORD while he may be found;
call to him while he is near.
⁷ Let the wicked one abandon his way
and the sinful one his thoughts;
let him return to the LORD,
so he may have compassion on him,
and to our God, for he will freely forgive.

⁸ "For my thoughts are not your thoughts,
and your ways are not my ways."
    This is the LORD's declaration.
⁹ "For as heaven is higher than earth,
so my ways are higher than your ways,
and my thoughts than your thoughts.
¹⁰ For just as rain and snow fall from heaven
and do not return there

NOTES

without saturating the earth
and making it germinate and sprout,
and providing seed to sow
and food to eat,
¹¹ so my word that comes from my mouth
will not return to me empty,
but it will accomplish what I please
and will prosper in what I send it to do."

¹² You will indeed go out with joy
and be peacefully guided;
the mountains and the hills will break into singing before you,
and all the trees of the field will clap their hands.
¹³ Instead of the thornbush, a cypress will come up,
and instead of the brier, a myrtle will come up;
this will stand as a monument for the LORD,
an everlasting sign that will not be destroyed.

◆ GOING DEEPER

HOSEA 14:1–3

A PLEA TO REPENT

¹ Israel, return to the LORD your God,
for you have stumbled in your iniquity.

² Take words of repentance with you
and return to the LORD.
Say to him, "Forgive all our iniquity
and accept what is good,
so that we may repay you
with praise from our lips.
³ Assyria will not save us,
we will not ride on horses,
and we will no longer proclaim, 'Our gods!'
to the work of our hands.
For the fatherless receives compassion in you."

MATTHEW 7:7–12

ASK, SEARCH, KNOCK

⁷ "Ask, and it will be given to you. Seek, and you will find. Knock, and the door will be opened to you. ⁸ For everyone who asks receives, and the one who seeks finds, and to the one who knocks, the door will be opened. ⁹ Who among you, if his son asks him for bread, will give him a stone? ¹⁰ Or if he asks for a fish, will give him a snake? ¹¹ If you then, who are evil, know how to give good gifts to your children, how much more will your Father in heaven give good things to those who ask him. ¹² Therefore, whatever you want others to do for you, do also the same for them, for this is the Law and the Prophets."

NOTES

WEEK FIVE
RESPONSE

USE THE FOLLOWING WORKSHEET TO HELP YOU REFLECT ON THIS WEEK'S READING.

Places or people the prophecies in this week's reading were directed toward:

An encouraging or challenging verse:

Isaiah :

A question to ponder and investigate:

Descriptive details about God and His people:

God

His People

How God's people were called to respond:

Specific sins revealed or warnings given:

GOD'S HOLINESS	How was God's holiness demonstrated in this week's reading? Circle one expression of His holiness in your answer above that stands out to you. How might trusting in this aspect of God strengthen your faith this Lenten season?
THE PEOPLE'S SIN	Review the sins that you listed on the previous page and consider how some of them may be present in your own life, even if they are expressed in different ways. Circle one that stands out to you and then use this space to reflect on the ways this sin appears in your own life.
HOPE FOR SALVATION THROUGH GOD	God responds to His people's sin and rebellion with a promise to save and restore them. Looking back on this week's reading, highlight or underline some of God's promises to His people. Having reflected on God's holiness and the reality of sin, how do these messages of hope encourage you as you journey through this season of Lent?

DAY 34

GRACE DAY

SECTION 2

Take this day to catch up on your reading, pray, and rest in the presence of the Lord.

IF WE CONFESS OUR SINS, HE IS FAITHFUL AND RIGHTEOUS TO FORGIVE US OUR SINS AND TO CLEANSE US FROM ALL UNRIGHTEOUSNESS.

1 JOHN 1:9

WEEKLY

DAY _____

Scripture is God breathed and true. When we memorize it, we carry His Word with us wherever we go.

During this reading plan, we have been memorizing our key verse, Isaiah 43:1. This week, we'll commit the entire verse to memory.

SEE TIPS FOR MEMORIZING SCRIPTURE ON PAGE 272.

———————————— 35   TRUTH

ISAIAH 43:1

Now this is what the Lord
says–the one who created you,
Jacob, and the one who formed
you, Israel–"Do not fear, for I
have redeemed you; I have called
you by your name; you are mine."

SECTION THREE

REPENTANCE
AND RESTORATION

ISAIAH 56–66

Isaiah 56-66 is the culmination of God's judgment and salvation. This section's call to repentance comes in response to how God had shown His character to His people through His just actions against Judah's sin and the comfort and healing He would extend after their judgment. These final chapters in Isaiah point to a future hope and restoration for God's nation and for all of creation. Thankfully, the hope for a better future found in these chapters remains true now, just as it did then.

When God's people repent and return to Him, they are given the glorious hope of restoration with their God and a new kind of kingdom, one built on God's compassion, love, and delight in His people. Chapter 65 contains one of the clearest depictions of the new creation, the place where God's people will dwell with Him and one another in perfect peace. In sharing this image, God both shows His will for the world and gives us a hope that will one day be our reality too.

DAY 36

HEALING AND PEACE

SECTION 3

ISAIAH 56

A HOUSE OF PRAYER FOR ALL

¹ This is what the Lord says:

Preserve justice and do what is right,
for my salvation is coming soon,
and my righteousness will be revealed.
² Happy is the person who does this,
the son of man who holds it fast,
who keeps the Sabbath without desecrating it,
and keeps his hand from doing any evil.

³ No foreigner who has joined himself to the Lord
should say,
"The Lord will exclude me from his people,"
and the eunuch should not say,
"Look, I am a dried-up tree."
⁴ For the Lord says this:
"For the eunuchs who keep my Sabbaths,
and choose what pleases me,
and hold firmly to my covenant,
⁵ I will give them, in my house and within my walls,
a memorial and a name
better than sons and daughters.
I will give each of them an everlasting name
that will never be cut off.
⁶ As for the foreigners who join themselves to the Lord
to minister to him, to love the name of the Lord,
and to become his servants—
all who keep the Sabbath without desecrating it
and who hold firmly to my covenant—
⁷ I will bring them to my holy mountain
and let them rejoice in my house of prayer.
Their burnt offerings and sacrifices
will be acceptable on my altar,
for my house will be called a house of prayer
for all nations."
⁸ This is the declaration of the Lord God,
who gathers the dispersed of Israel:
"I will gather to them still others
besides those already gathered."

NOTES

UNRIGHTEOUS LEADERS CONDEMNED

⁹ All you animals of the field and forest,
come and eat!
¹⁰ Israel's watchmen are blind, all of them,
they know nothing;
all of them are mute dogs,
they cannot bark;
they dream, lie down,
and love to sleep.
¹¹ These dogs have fierce appetites;
they never have enough.
And they are shepherds
who have no discernment;
all of them turn to their own way,
every last one for his own profit.
¹² "Come, let me get some wine,
let's guzzle some beer;
and tomorrow will be like today,
only far better!"

ISAIAH 57

¹ The righteous person perishes,
and no one takes it to heart;
the faithful are taken away,
with no one realizing
that the righteous person is taken away
because of evil.

² He will enter into peace—
they will rest on their beds—
everyone who lives uprightly.

PAGAN RELIGION DENOUNCED

³ But come here,
you witch's sons,
offspring of an adulterer and a prostitute!
⁴ Who are you mocking?
Who are you opening your mouth

and sticking out your tongue at?
Isn't it you, you rebellious children,
you offspring of liars,
⁵ who burn with lust among the oaks,
under every green tree,
who slaughter children in the wadis
below the clefts of the rocks?
⁶ Your portion is among the smooth stones of the wadi;
indeed, they are your lot.
You have even poured out a drink offering to them;
you have offered a grain offering;
should I be satisfied with these?
⁷ You have placed your bed
on a high and lofty mountain;
you also went up there to offer sacrifice.
⁸ You have set up your memorial
behind the door and doorpost.
For away from me, you stripped,
went up, and made your bed wide,
and you have made a bargain for yourself with them.
You have loved their bed;
you have gazed on their genitals.
⁹ You went to the king with oil
and multiplied your perfumes;
you sent your envoys far away
and sent them down even to Sheol.
¹⁰ You became weary on your many journeys,
but you did not say, "It's hopeless!"
You found a renewal of your strength;
therefore you did not grow weak.
¹¹ Who was it you dreaded and feared,
so that you lied and didn't remember me
or take it to heart?
I have kept silent for a long time, haven't I?
So you do not fear me.
¹² I will announce your righteousness,
and your works—they will not profit you.

¹³ When you cry out,
let your collection of idols rescue you!

NOTES

The wind will carry all of them off,
a breath will take them away.
But whoever takes refuge in me
will inherit the land
and possess my holy mountain.

HEALING AND PEACE

[14] He said,
"Build it up, build it up, prepare the way,
remove every obstacle from my people's way."
[15] For the High and Exalted One,
who lives forever, whose name is holy, says this:
"I live in a high and holy place,
and with the oppressed and lowly of spirit,
to revive the spirit of the lowly
and revive the heart of the oppressed.
[16] For I will not accuse you forever,
and I will not always be angry;
for then the spirit would grow weak before me,
even the breath, which I have made.
[17] Because of his sinful greed I was angry,
so I struck him; I was angry and hid;
but he went on turning back to the desires of his heart.
[18] I have seen his ways, but I will heal him;
I will lead him and restore comfort
to him and his mourners,
[19] creating words of praise."
The LORD says,
"Peace, peace to the one who is far or near,
and I will heal him.
[20] But the wicked are like the storm-tossed sea,
for it cannot be still,
and its water churns up mire and muck.
[21] There is no peace for the wicked,"
says my God.

GOING DEEPER

PSALM 103:1–13

THE FORGIVING GOD

Of David.

¹ My soul, bless the Lord,
and all that is within me, bless his holy name.
² My soul, bless the Lord,
and do not forget all his benefits.

³ He forgives all your iniquity;
he heals all your diseases.
⁴ He redeems your life from the Pit;
he crowns you with faithful love and compassion.
⁵ He satisfies you with good things;
your youth is renewed like the eagle.

⁶ The Lord executes acts of righteousness
and justice for all the oppressed.
⁷ He revealed his ways to Moses,
his deeds to the people of Israel.
⁸ The Lord is compassionate and gracious,
slow to anger and abounding in faithful love.
⁹ He will not always accuse us
or be angry forever.
¹⁰ He has not dealt with us as our sins deserve
or repaid us according to our iniquities.

¹¹ For as high as the heavens are above the earth,
so great is his faithful love
toward those who fear him.
¹² As far as the east is from the west,
so far has he removed
our transgressions from us.
¹³ As a father has compassion on his children,
so the Lord has compassion on those who fear him.

THE LORD'S GLORY IN ZION

DAY 37   SECTION 3

ISAIAH 58

TRUE FASTING

¹ "Cry out loudly, don't hold back!
Raise your voice like a ram's horn.
Tell my people their transgression
and the house of Jacob their sins.
² They seek me day after day
and delight to know my ways,
like a nation that does what is right
and does not abandon the justice of
    their God.
They ask me for righteous judgments;
they delight in the nearness of God."

³ "Why have we fasted, but you have
    not seen?
We have denied ourselves, but you
    haven't noticed!"

"Look, you do as you please on the day of
    your fast,
and oppress all your workers.
⁴ You fast with contention and strife
to strike viciously with your fist.
You cannot fast as you do today,
hoping to make your voice heard on high.
⁵ Will the fast I choose be like this:
A day for a person to deny himself,
to bow his head like a reed,

and to spread out sackcloth and ashes?
Will you call this a fast
and a day acceptable to the LORD?
⁶ Isn't this the fast I choose:
To break the chains of wickedness,
to untie the ropes of the yoke,
to set the oppressed free,
and to tear off every yoke?
⁷ Is it not to share your bread with
    the hungry,
to bring the poor and homeless into
    your house,
to clothe the naked when you see him,
and not to ignore your own flesh and blood?
⁸ Then your light will appear like the dawn,
and your recovery will come quickly.
Your righteousness will go before you,
and the LORD's glory will be your rear guard.

⁹ At that time, when you call, the LORD
will answer;
when you cry out, he will say, 'Here I am.'
If you get rid of the yoke among you,
the finger-pointing and malicious speaking,
¹⁰ and if you offer yourself to the hungry,
and satisfy the afflicted one,
then your light will shine in the darkness,

and your night will be like noonday.
¹¹ The Lord will always lead you,
satisfy you in a parched land,
and strengthen your bones.
You will be like a watered garden
and like a spring whose water never runs dry.
¹² Some of you will rebuild the ancient ruins;
you will restore the foundations laid long ago;
you will be called the repairer of broken walls,
the restorer of streets where people live.
¹³ "If you keep from desecrating the Sabbath,
from doing whatever you want on my holy day;
if you call the Sabbath a delight,
and the holy day of the Lord honorable;
if you honor it, not going your own ways,
seeking your own pleasure, or talking business;
¹⁴ then you will delight in the Lord,
and I will make you ride over the heights of the land,
and let you enjoy the heritage of your father Jacob."
For the mouth of the Lord has spoken.

ISAIAH 59

SIN AND REDEMPTION

¹ Indeed, the Lord's arm is not too weak to save,
and his ear is not too deaf to hear.
² But your iniquities are separating you
from your God,
and your sins have hidden his face from you
so that he does not listen.
³ For your hands are defiled with blood
and your fingers, with iniquity;
your lips have spoken lies,
and your tongues mutter injustice.
⁴ No one makes claims justly;
no one pleads honestly.
They trust in empty and worthless words;
they conceive trouble and give birth to iniquity.
⁵ They hatch viper's eggs
and weave spider's webs.
Whoever eats their eggs will die;

crack one open, and a viper is hatched.
⁶ Their webs cannot become clothing,
and they cannot cover themselves with
    their works.
Their works are sinful works,
and violent acts are in their hands.
⁷ Their feet run after evil,
and they rush to shed innocent blood.
Their thoughts are sinful thoughts;
ruin and wretchedness are in their paths.

⁸ They have not known the path of peace,
and there is no justice in their ways.
They have made their roads crooked;
no one who walks on them will know peace.
⁹ Therefore justice is far from us,
and righteousness does not reach us.
We hope for light, but there is darkness;
for brightness, but we live in the night.
¹⁰ We grope along a wall like the blind;
we grope like those without eyes.
We stumble at noon as though it
    were twilight;
we are like the dead among those who
    are healthy.
¹¹ We all growl like bears
and moan like doves.
We hope for justice, but there is none;
for salvation, but it is far from us.
¹² For our transgressions have multiplied
    before you,
and our sins testify against us.
For our transgressions are with us,
and we know our iniquities:
¹³ transgression and deception against
    the Lord,
turning away from following our God,
speaking oppression and revolt,
conceiving and uttering lying words from
    the heart.

¹⁴ Justice is turned back,
and righteousness stands far off.
For truth has stumbled in the public square,
and honesty cannot enter.
¹⁵ Truth is missing,
and whoever turns from evil is plundered.
The Lord saw that there was no justice,
and he was offended.
¹⁶ He saw that there was no man—
he was amazed that there was no
    one interceding;
so his own arm brought salvation,
and his own righteousness supported him.

¹⁷ He put on righteousness as body armor,
and a helmet of salvation on his head;
he put on garments of vengeance
    for clothing,
and he wrapped himself in zeal as in a cloak.
¹⁸ So he will repay according to their deeds:
fury to his enemies,
retribution to his foes,
and he will repay the coasts and islands.
¹⁹ They will fear the name of the Lord in
    the west
and his glory in the east;
for he will come like a rushing stream
driven by the wind of the Lord.
²⁰ "The Redeemer will come to Zion,
and to those in Jacob who turn
    from transgression."
This is the Lord's declaration.

²¹ "As for me, this is my covenant with them," says the Lord: "My Spirit who is on you, and my words that I have put in your mouth, will not depart from your mouth, or from the mouths of your children, or from the mouths of your children's children, from now on and forever," says the Lord.

ISAIAH 60

THE LORD'S GLORY IN ZION

¹ Arise, shine, for your light has come,
and the glory of the Lord shines over you.
² For look, darkness will cover the earth,
and total darkness the peoples;
but the Lord will shine over you,
and his glory will appear over you.
³ Nations will come to your light,
and kings to your shining brightness.

⁴ Raise your eyes and look around:
they all gather and come to you;
your sons will come from far away,
and your daughters on the hips of nursing mothers.
⁵ Then you will see and be radiant,
and your heart will tremble and rejoice,
because the riches of the sea will become yours
and the wealth of the nations will come to you.
⁶ Caravans of camels will cover your land—
young camels of Midian and Ephah—
all of them will come from Sheba.
They will carry gold and frankincense
and proclaim the praises of the Lord.
⁷ All the flocks of Kedar will be gathered to you;
the rams of Nebaioth will serve you
and go up on my altar as an acceptable sacrifice.
I will glorify my beautiful house.

⁸ Who are these who fly like a cloud,
like doves to their shelters?
⁹ Yes, the coasts and islands will wait for me
with the ships of Tarshish in the lead,
to bring your children from far away,
their silver and gold with them,
for the honor of the Lord your God,
the Holy One of Israel,
who has glorified you.

NOTES

¹⁰ Foreigners will rebuild your walls,
and their kings will serve you.
Although I struck you in my wrath,
yet I will show mercy to you with my favor.
¹¹ Your city gates will always be open;
they will never be shut day or night
so that the wealth of the nations
may be brought into you,
with their kings being led in procession.
¹² For the nation and the kingdom
that will not serve you will perish;
those nations will be annihilated.
¹³ The glory of Lebanon will come to you—
its pine, elm, and cypress together—
to beautify the place of my sanctuary,
and I will glorify my dwelling place.
¹⁴ The sons of your oppressors
will come and bow down to you;
all who reviled you
will fall facedown at your feet.
They will call you the City of the Lord,
Zion of the Holy One of Israel.
¹⁵ Instead of your being deserted and hated,
with no one passing through,
I will make you an object of eternal pride,
a joy from age to age.
¹⁶ You will nurse on the milk of nations,
and nurse at the breast of kings;
you will know that I, the Lord, am your Savior
and Redeemer, the Mighty One of Jacob.
¹⁷ I will bring gold instead of bronze;
I will bring silver instead of iron,
bronze instead of wood,
and iron instead of stones.
I will appoint peace as your government
and righteousness as your overseers.
¹⁸ Violence will never again be heard of in your land;
devastation and destruction
will be gone from your borders.
You will call your walls Salvation
and your city gates Praise.

¹⁹ The sun will no longer be your light by day,
and the brightness of the moon will not shine on you.
The Lord will be your everlasting light,
and your God will be your splendor.
²⁰ Your sun will no longer set,
and your moon will not fade;
for the Lord will be your everlasting light,
and the days of your sorrow will be over.

²¹ All your people will be righteous;
they will possess the land forever;
they are the branch I planted,
the work of my hands,
so that I may be glorified.

²² The least will become a thousand,
the smallest a mighty nation.
I am the Lord;
I will accomplish it quickly in its time.

GOING DEEPER

REVELATION 21:22-27

²² I did not see a temple in it, because the Lord God the Almighty and the Lamb are its temple. ²³ The city does not need the sun or the moon to shine on it, because the glory of God illuminates it, and its lamp is the Lamb. ²⁴ The nations will walk by its light, and the kings of the earth will bring their glory into it. ²⁵ Its gates will never close by day because it will never be night there. ²⁶ They will bring the glory and honor of the nations into it. ²⁷ Nothing unclean will ever enter it, nor anyone who does what is detestable or false, but only those written in the Lamb's book of life.

ZION'S RESTORATION

DAY 38 — SECTION 3

ISAIAH 61

MESSIAH'S JUBILEE

¹ The Spirit of the Lord God is on me,
because the Lord has anointed me
to bring good news to the poor.
He has sent me to heal the brokenhearted,
to proclaim liberty to the captives
and freedom to the prisoners;
² to proclaim the year of the Lord's favor,
and the day of our God's vengeance;
to comfort all who mourn,
³ to provide for those who mourn in Zion;
to give them a crown of beauty instead
    of ashes,
festive oil instead of mourning,
and splendid clothes instead of despair.
And they will be called righteous trees,
planted by the Lord
to glorify him.
⁴ They will rebuild the ancient ruins;
they will restore the former devastations;
they will renew the ruined cities,
the devastations of many generations.
⁵ Strangers will stand and feed your flocks,
and foreigners will be your plowmen
    and vinedressers.

⁶ But you will be called the Lord's priests;
they will speak of you as ministers of
    our God;
you will eat the wealth of the nations,
and you will boast in their riches.
⁷ In place of your shame, you will have a
    double portion;
in place of disgrace, they will rejoice over
    their share.
So they will possess double in their land,
and eternal joy will be theirs.

⁸ For I the Lord love justice;
I hate robbery and injustice;
I will faithfully reward my people

and make a permanent covenant with them.
⁹ Their descendants will be known among
    the nations,
and their posterity among the peoples.
All who see them will recognize
that they are a people the Lord has blessed.

¹⁰ I rejoice greatly in the Lord,
I exult in my God;
for he has clothed me with the garments
    of salvation
and wrapped me in a robe of righteousness,
as a groom wears a turban
and as a bride adorns herself with her jewels.
¹¹ For as the earth produces its growth,
and as a garden enables what is sown to
    spring up,
so the Lord God will cause righteousness
    and praise
to spring up before all the nations.

ISAIAH 62

ZION'S RESTORATION

¹ I will not keep silent because of Zion,
and I will not keep still because of Jerusalem,
until her righteousness shines like a
    bright light
and her salvation, like a flaming torch.

² Nations will see your righteousness
and all kings, your glory.
You will be given a new name
that the Lord's mouth will announce.

³ You will be a glorious crown in the
    Lord's hand,
and a royal diadem in the palm of your
    God's hand.
⁴ You will no longer be called Deserted,
and your land will not be called Desolate;
instead, you will be called My Delight Is
    in Her,
and your land Married;
for the Lord delights in you,
and your land will be married.
⁵ For as a young man marries a
    young woman,
so your sons will marry you;
and as a groom rejoices over his bride,
so your God will rejoice over you.
⁶ Jerusalem,
I have appointed watchmen on your walls;
they will never be silent, day or night.
There is no rest for you,
who remind the Lord.
⁷ Do not give him rest
until he establishes and makes Jerusalem
the praise of the earth.

⁸ The Lord has sworn with his right hand
and his strong arm:
I will no longer give your grain
to your enemies for food,
and foreigners will not drink the new wine
for which you have labored.
⁹ For those who gather grain will eat it
and praise the Lord,
and those who harvest the grapes will drink
    the wine
in my holy courts.
¹⁰ Go out, go out through the city gates;
prepare a way for the people!
Build it up, build up the highway;
clear away the stones!
Raise a banner for the peoples.
¹¹ Look, the Lord has proclaimed
to the ends of the earth,
"Say to Daughter Zion:
Look, your salvation is coming,
his wages are with him,
and his reward accompanies him."

¹² And they will be called the Holy People,
the Lord's Redeemed;
and you will be called Cared For,
A City Not Deserted.

GOING DEEPER

LUKE 4:16-21

REJECTION AT NAZARETH

¹⁶ He came to Nazareth, where he had been brought up. As usual, he entered the synagogue on the Sabbath day and stood up to read. ¹⁷ The scroll of the prophet Isaiah was given to him, and unrolling the scroll, he found the place where it was written:

¹⁸ The Spirit of the Lord is on me,
because he has anointed me
to preach good news to the poor.
He has sent me
to proclaim release to the captives
and recovery of sight to the blind,
to set free the oppressed,
¹⁹ to proclaim the year of the Lord's favor.

²⁰ He then rolled up the scroll, gave it back to the attendant, and sat down. And the eyes of everyone in the synagogue were fixed on him. ²¹ He began by saying to them, "Today as you listen, this Scripture has been fulfilled."

1 PETER 2:9-10

⁹ But you are a chosen race, a royal priesthood, a holy nation, a people for his possession, so that you may proclaim the praises of the one who called you out of darkness into his marvelous light.

¹⁰ Once you were not a people, but now you are God's people; you had not received mercy, but now you have received mercy.

PROPHECIES FROM ISAIAH
FULFILLED IN JESUS

The book of Isaiah contains more than thirty-five messianic prophecies that we can see fulfilled in the New Testament. Here are some of Isaiah's prophecies about the coming Messiah and an example of how the New Testament points to how it has been fulfilled through Jesus.

• TOPIC	• PROPHECY	• FULFILLMENT
Born of a virgin	Therefore, the Lord himself will give you a sign: See, the virgin will conceive, have a son, and name him Immanuel. *Is 7:14*	Now all this took place to fulfill what was spoken by the Lord through the prophet: See, the virgin will become pregnant and give birth to a son, and they will name him Immanuel, which is translated "God is with us." When Joseph woke up, he did as the Lord's angel had commanded him… *Mt 1:22–24*
Hearers with hard hearts	And he replied: Go! Say to these people: Keep listening, but do not understand; keep looking, but do not perceive. *Is 6:9*	For this people's heart has grown callous; their ears are hard of hearing, and they have shut their eyes; otherwise they might see with their eyes, and hear with their ears, and understand with their hearts, and turn back— and I would heal them. *Mt 13:15*
Heir to David's throne	The dominion will be vast, and its prosperity will never end. He will reign on the throne of David and over his kingdom, to establish and sustain it with justice and righteousness from now on and forever. The zeal of the Lord of Armies will accomplish this. *Is 9:7*	Then the angel told her: "Do not be afraid, Mary, for you have found favor with God. Now listen: You will conceive and give birth to a son, and you will name him Jesus. He will be great and will be called the Son of the Most High, and the Lord God will give him the throne of his father David." *Lk 1:30–32*

• TOPIC	• PROPHECY	• FULFILLMENT
God's Spirit	The Spirit of the LORD will rest on him— a Spirit of wisdom and understanding, a Spirit of counsel and strength, a Spirit of knowledge and of the fear of the LORD. *Is 11:2*	As soon as he came up out of the water, he saw the heavens being torn open and the Spirit descending on him like a dove. *Mk 1:10*
Would make the lame walk	Then the lame will leap like a deer, and the tongue of the mute will sing for joy, for water will gush in the wilderness, and streams in the desert… *Is 35:6*	"But so that you may know that the Son of Man has authority on earth to forgive sins"—he told the paralytic—"I tell you: get up, take your mat, and go home." Immediately he got up, took the mat, and went out in front of everyone. As a result, they were all astounded and gave glory to God, saying, "We have never seen anything like this!" *Mk 2:10-12*
The way prepared	A voice of one crying out: Prepare the way of the LORD in the wilderness; make a straight highway for our God in the desert. *Is 40:3*	"Who are you, then?" they asked. "We need to give an answer to those who sent us. What can you tell us about yourself?" [John the Baptist] said, "I am a voice of one crying out in the wilderness: Make straight the way of the Lord—just as Isaiah the prophet said." *Jn 1:22-23*
Rejected	He was despised and rejected by men, a man of suffering who knew what sickness was. He was like someone people turned away from; he was despised, and we didn't value him. *Is 53:3*	He came to his own, and his own people did not receive him. *Jn 1:11*

 • TOPIC	 • PROPHECY	 • FULFILLMENT
Crucified with sinners	Therefore I will give him the many as a portion, and he will receive the mighty as spoil, because he willingly submitted to death, and was counted among the rebels; yet he bore the sin of many and interceded for the rebels. *Is 53:12*	They crucified two criminals with him, one on his right and one on his left. *Mk 15:27*
Wounded healer	But he was pierced because of our rebellion, crushed because of our iniquities; punishment for our peace was on him, and we are healed by his wounds. *Is 53:5*	He himself bore our sins in his body on the tree; so that, having died to sins, we might live for righteousness. By his wounds you have been healed. *1Pt 2:24*
Silent in oppression	He was oppressed and afflicted, yet he did not open his mouth. Like a lamb led to the slaughter and like a sheep silent before her shearers, he did not open his mouth. *Is 53:7*	The high priest stood up and said to him, "Don't you have an answer to what these men are testifying against you?" But Jesus kept silent. The high priest said to him, "I charge you under oath by the living God: Tell us if you are the Messiah, the Son of God." *Mt 26:62-63*

ISRAEL'S PRAYER

———

LORD, DO NOT BE TERRIBLY ANGRY
OR REMEMBER OUR INIQUITY
FOREVER. PLEASE LOOK—ALL OF
US ARE YOUR PEOPLE!

ISAIAH 64:9

DAY 39   SECTION 3

ISAIAH 63

THE LORD'S DAY OF VENGEANCE

¹ Who is this coming from Edom
in crimson-stained garments from Bozrah—
this one who is splendid in his apparel,
striding in his formidable might?
It is I, proclaiming vindication,
powerful to save.
² Why are your clothes red,
and your garments like one who treads a winepress?
³ I trampled the winepress alone,
and no one from the nations was with me.
I trampled them in my anger
and ground them underfoot in my fury;
their blood spattered my garments,
and all my clothes were stained.
⁴ For I planned the day of vengeance,
and the year of my redemption came.

⁵ I looked, but there was no one to help,
and I was amazed that no one assisted;
so my arm accomplished victory for me,
and my wrath assisted me.

⁶ I crushed nations in my anger;
I made them drunk with my wrath
and poured out their blood on the ground.

REMEMBRANCE OF GRACE

⁷ I will make known the LORD's faithful love
and the LORD's praiseworthy acts,
because of all the LORD has done for us—
even the many good things
he has done for the house of Israel,
which he did for them based on his compassion
and the abundance of his faithful love.
⁸ He said, "They are indeed my people,
children who will not be disloyal,"
and he became their Savior.

NOTES

⁹ In all their suffering, he suffered,
and the angel of his presence saved them.

> He redeemed them
> because of his love and compassion;
> he lifted them up and carried them
> all the days of the past.

¹⁰ But they rebelled
and grieved his Holy Spirit.
So he became their enemy
and fought against them.
¹¹ Then he remembered the days of the past,
the days of Moses and his people.
Where is he who brought them out of the sea
with the shepherds of his flock?
Where is he who put his Holy Spirit among the flock?
¹² He made his glorious strength
available at the right hand of Moses,
divided the water before them
to make an eternal name for himself,
¹³ and led them through the depths
like a horse in the wilderness,
so that they did not stumble.

¹⁴ Like cattle that go down into the valley,
the Spirit of the Lord gave them rest.
You led your people this way
to make a glorious name for yourself.

ISRAEL'S PRAYER

¹⁵ Look down from heaven and see
from your lofty home—holy and beautiful.
Where is your zeal and your might?
Your yearning and your compassion
are withheld from me.
¹⁶ Yet you are our Father,
even though Abraham does not know us
and Israel doesn't recognize us.

You, LORD, are our Father;
your name is Our Redeemer
from Ancient Times.
¹⁷ Why, LORD, do you make us stray from your ways?
You harden our hearts so we do not fear you.
Return, because of your servants,
the tribes of your heritage.
¹⁸ Your holy people had a possession
for a little while,
but our enemies have trampled down
your sanctuary.
¹⁹ We have become like those you never ruled,
like those who did not bear your name.

ISAIAH 64

¹ If only you would tear the heavens open
and come down,
so that mountains would quake at your presence—
² just as fire kindles brushwood,
and fire boils water—
to make your name known to your enemies,
so that nations would tremble at your presence!
³ When you did awesome works
that we did not expect,
you came down,
and the mountains quaked at your presence.
⁴ From ancient times no one has heard,
no one has listened to,
no eye has seen any God except you
who acts on behalf of the one who waits for him.
⁵ You welcome the one who joyfully does what is right;
they remember you in your ways.
But we have sinned, and you were angry.
How can we be saved if we remain in our sins?
⁶ All of us have become like something unclean,
and all our righteous acts are like a polluted garment;
all of us wither like a leaf,
and our iniquities carry us away like the wind.

NOTES

NOTES

⁷ No one calls on your name,
striving to take hold of you.
For you have hidden your face from us
and made us melt because of our iniquity.

⁸ Yet Lord, you are our Father;
we are the clay, and you are our potter;
we all are the work of your hands.

⁹ Lord, do not be terribly angry
or remember our iniquity forever.
Please look—all of us are your people!
¹⁰ Your holy cities have become a wilderness;
Zion has become a wilderness,
Jerusalem a desolation.
¹¹ Our holy and beautiful temple,
where our ancestors praised you,
has been burned down,
and all that was dear to us lies in ruins.
¹² Lord, after all this, will you restrain yourself?
Will you keep silent and afflict us severely?

◆ GOING DEEPER

MICAH 7:18–20

¹⁸ Who is a God like you,
forgiving iniquity and passing over rebellion
for the remnant of his inheritance?
He does not hold on to his anger forever
because he delights in faithful love.
¹⁹ He will again have compassion on us;
he will vanquish our iniquities.
You will cast all our sins
into the depths of the sea.
²⁰ You will show loyalty to Jacob
and faithful love to Abraham,
as you swore to our ancestors
from days long ago.

PHILIPPIANS 3:18-21

[18] For I have often told you, and now say again with tears, that many live as enemies of the cross of Christ. [19] Their end is destruction; their god is their stomach; their glory is in their shame; and they are focused on earthly things. [20] Our citizenship is in heaven, and we eagerly wait for a Savior from there, the Lord Jesus Christ. [21] He will transform the body of our humble condition into the likeness of his glorious body, by the power that enables him to subject everything to himself.

DAY 40 · SECTION 3

JOYOUS RESTORATION

ISAIAH 65

THE LORD'S RESPONSE

¹ "I was sought by those who did not ask;
I was found by those who did not seek me.
I said, 'Here I am, here I am,'
to a nation that did not call on my name.
² I spread out my hands all day long
to a rebellious people
who walk in the path that is not good,
following their own thoughts.
³ These people continually anger me
to my face,
sacrificing in gardens,
burning incense on bricks,
⁴ sitting among the graves,
spending nights in secret places,
eating the meat of pigs,
and putting polluted broth in their bowls.
⁵ They say, 'Keep to yourself,
don't come near me, for I am too holy for you!'
These practices are smoke in my nostrils,
a fire that burns all day long.
⁶ Look, it is written in front of me:
I will not keep silent, but I will repay;
I will repay them fully
⁷ for your iniquities and the iniquities

of your ancestors together,"
says the L ORD.
"Because they burned incense on the mountains
and reproached me on the hills,
I will reward them fully
for their former deeds."

⁸ The L ORD says this:

"As the new wine is found in a bunch of grapes,
and one says, 'Don't destroy it,
for there's some good in it,'
so I will act because of my servants
and not destroy them all.
⁹ I will produce descendants from Jacob,
and heirs to my mountains from Judah;
my chosen ones will possess it,
and my servants will dwell there.
¹⁰ Sharon will be a pasture for flocks,
and the Valley of Achor a place for herds to lie down,
for my people who have sought me.
¹¹ But you who abandon the L ORD,
who forget my holy mountain,
who prepare a table for Fortune
and fill bowls of mixed wine for Destiny,
¹² I will destine you for the sword,
and all of you will kneel down to be slaughtered,
because I called and you did not answer,
I spoke and you did not hear;
you did what was evil in my sight
and chose what I did not delight in."

¹³ Therefore, this is what the Lord G OD says:

"Look! My servants will eat,
but you will be hungry.
Look! My servants will drink,
but you will be thirsty.
Look! My servants will rejoice,
but you will be put to shame.
¹⁴ Look! My servants will shout for joy from a glad heart,
but you will cry out from an anguished heart,

and you will lament out of a broken spirit.
¹⁵ You will leave your name behind
as a curse for my chosen ones,
and the Lord God will kill you;
but he will give his servants another name.
¹⁶ Whoever asks for a blessing in the land
will ask for a blessing by the God of truth,
and whoever swears in the land
will swear by the God of truth.
For the former troubles will be forgotten
and hidden from my sight.

A NEW CREATION

¹⁷ "For I will create new heavens and a
    new earth;
the past events will not be remembered or
    come to mind.
¹⁸ Then be glad and rejoice forever
in what I am creating;
for I will create Jerusalem to be a joy
and its people to be a delight.
¹⁹ I will rejoice in Jerusalem
and be glad in my people.
The sound of weeping and crying
will no longer be heard in her.
²⁰ In her, a nursing infant will no longer live
only a few days,
or an old man not live out his days.
Indeed, the one who dies at a hundred
    years old
will be mourned as a young man,
and the one who misses a hundred years
will be considered cursed.
²¹ People will build houses and live in them;
they will plant vineyards and eat their fruit.
²² They will not build and others live
    in them;
they will not plant and others eat.
For my people's lives will be
like the lifetime of a tree.
My chosen ones will fully enjoy
the work of their hands.
²³ They will not labor without success
or bear children destined for disaster,
for they will be a people blessed by the Lord
along with their descendants.
²⁴ Even before they call, I will answer;
while they are still speaking, I will hear.
²⁵ The wolf and the lamb will feed together,
and the lion will eat straw like cattle,
but the serpent's food will be dust!
They will not do what is evil or destroy
on my entire holy mountain,"
says the Lord.

ISAIAH 66

FINAL JUDGMENT AND
JOYOUS RESTORATION

¹ This is what the Lord says:

Heaven is my throne,
and earth is my footstool.
Where could you possibly build a house
    for me?
And where would my resting place be?
² My hand made all these things,
and so they all came into being.
    This is the Lord's declaration.
I will look favorably on this kind of person:
one who is humble, submissive in spirit,
and trembles at my word.
³ One person slaughters an ox, another kills
    a person;
one person sacrifices a lamb, another breaks
    a dog's neck;
one person offers a grain offering, another
    offers pig's blood;
one person offers incense, another praises
    an idol—
all these have chosen their ways
and delight in their abhorrent practices.

⁴ So I will choose their punishment,
and I will bring on them what they dread
because I called and no one answered;
I spoke and they did not listen;
they did what was evil in my sight
and chose what I did not delight in.
⁵ You who tremble at his word,
hear the word of the Lord:
"Your brothers who hate and exclude you
for my name's sake have said,
'Let the Lord be glorified
so that we can see your joy!'
But they will be put to shame."
⁶ A sound of uproar from the city!
A voice from the temple—
the voice of the Lord,
paying back his enemies what they deserve!
⁷ Before Zion was in labor, she gave birth;
before she was in pain, she delivered a boy.
⁸ Who has heard of such a thing?
Who has seen such things?
Can a land be born in one day
or a nation be delivered in an instant?
Yet as soon as Zion was in labor,
she gave birth to her sons.
⁹ "Will I bring a baby to the point of birth
and not deliver it?"
says the Lord;
"or will I who deliver, close the womb?"
says your God.
¹⁰ Be glad for Jerusalem and rejoice over her,
all who love her.
Rejoice greatly with her,
all who mourn over her—
¹¹ so that you may nurse and be satisfied
from her comforting breast
and drink deeply and delight yourselves
from her glorious breasts.

¹² For this is what the Lord says:

NOTES

NOTES

I will make peace flow to her like a river,
and the wealth of nations like a flood;
you will nurse and be carried on her hip
and bounced on her lap.
[13] As a mother comforts her son,
so I will comfort you,
and you will be comforted in Jerusalem.
[14] You will see, you will rejoice,
and you will flourish like grass;
then the Lord's power will be revealed to his servants,
but he will show his wrath against his enemies.
[15] Look, the Lord will come with fire—
his chariots are like the whirlwind—
to execute his anger with fury
and his rebuke with flames of fire.
[16] For the Lord will execute judgment
on all humanity with his fiery sword,
and many will be slain by the Lord.

[17] "Those who dedicate and purify themselves to enter the groves following their leader, eating meat from pigs, vermin, and rats, will perish together."

This is the Lord's declaration.

[18] "Knowing their works and their thoughts, I have come to gather all nations and languages; they will come and see my glory. [19] I will establish a sign among them, and I will send survivors from them to the nations—to Tarshish, Put, Lud (who are archers), Tubal, Javan, and the coasts and islands far away—who have not heard about me or seen my glory. And they will proclaim my glory among the nations. [20] They will bring all your brothers from all the nations as a gift to the Lord on horses and chariots, in litters, and on mules and camels, to my holy mountain Jerusalem," says the Lord, "just as the Israelites bring an offering in a clean vessel to the house of the Lord. [21] I will also take some of them as priests and Levites," says the Lord.

[22] "For just as the new heavens and the new earth,
which I will make,
will remain before me"—
 this is the Lord's declaration—

"so your offspring and your name will remain.
²³ All humanity will come to worship me
from one New Moon to another
and from one Sabbath to another,"
says the LORD.

²⁴ "As they leave, they will see the dead bodies of those who have rebelled against me; for their worm will never die, their fire will never go out, and they will be a horror to all humanity."

◼ GOING DEEPER

ROMANS 8:19-25

¹⁹ For the creation eagerly waits with anticipation for God's sons to be revealed. ²⁰ For the creation was subjected to futility—not willingly, but because of him who subjected it—in the hope ²¹ that the creation itself will also be set free from the bondage to decay into the glorious freedom of God's children. ²² For we know that the whole creation has been groaning together with labor pains until now. ²³ Not only that, but we ourselves who have the Spirit as the firstfruits—we also groan within ourselves, eagerly waiting for adoption, the redemption of our bodies. ²⁴ Now in this hope we were saved, but hope that is seen is not hope, because who hopes for what he sees? ²⁵ Now if we hope for what we do not see, we eagerly wait for it with patience.

REVELATION 21:1-4

THE NEW CREATION

¹ Then I saw a new heaven and a new earth; for the first heaven and the first earth had passed away, and the sea was no more. ² I also saw the holy city, the new Jerusalem, coming down out of heaven from God, prepared like a bride adorned for her husband.

³ Then I heard a loud voice from the throne: Look, God's dwelling is with humanity, and he will live with them. They will be his peoples, and God himself will be with them and will be their God. ⁴ He will wipe away every tear from their eyes. Death will be no more; grief, crying, and pain will be no more, because the previous things have passed away.

WEEK SIX
RESPONSE

USE THE FOLLOWING WORKSHEET TO HELP YOU REFLECT ON THIS WEEK'S READING.

Places or people the prophecies in this week's reading were directed toward:

An encouraging or challenging verse:

Isaiah :

A question to ponder and investigate:

Descriptive details about God and His people:

God

His People

Specific sins revealed or warnings given:

How God's people were called to respond:

PRAYER

Throughout our reading of Isaiah, we have reflected each week on God's holiness, our sin, and the hope of salvation. Use this space to respond in prayer as you move through the Lenten season into Holy Week. As you write, praise God for the expressions of His holiness you noticed in Isaiah, confess and repent of any sin that has been revealed in your life, and give thanks for the hope we have because of our salvation through Christ.

DAY 41

GRACE DAY

SECTION 3

Take this day to catch up on your reading, pray, and rest in the presence of the Lord.

ONCE YOU WERE NOT A PEOPLE, BUT NOW YOU ARE GOD'S PEOPLE; YOU HAD NOT RECEIVED MERCY, BUT NOW YOU HAVE RECEIVED MERCY.

1 PETER 2:10

HOLY WEEK

SECTION FOUR

At the start of Holy Week, there is an air of anticipation. Like the book of Isaiah, it is somber and hopeful, woe-filled and encouraging, heartbreaking and healing. We see opposites paired together in the experiences before Jesus's resurrection too–the dissent of the Pharisees and the praise of the crowds, meals with His betrayer and closest friends, a gruesome death and a glorious resurrection.

Keep the message of Isaiah in mind through the last week of our Lenten reading plan as we go through the final week of Jesus's life on earth. While we read of how He entered Jerusalem on a humble donkey, carried His own cross to the site of His death, and emerged from the tomb in victory, remember **Jesus endured all of this so that He could give us "a crown of beauty instead of ashes, festive oil instead of mourning, and splendid clothes instead of despair" (Is 61:3).**

PALM SUNDAY

DAY 42 — SECTION 4

LUKE 19:28-44

THE TRIUMPHAL ENTRY

[28] When he had said these things, he went on ahead, going up to Jerusalem. [29] As he approached Bethphage and Bethany, at the place called the Mount of Olives, he sent two of the disciples [30] and said, "Go into the village ahead of you. As you enter it, you will find a colt tied there, on which no one has ever sat. Untie it and bring it. [31] If anyone asks you, 'Why are you untying it?' say this: 'The Lord needs it.'"

[32] So those who were sent left and found it just as he had told them. [33] As they were untying the colt, its owners said to them, "Why are you untying the colt?"

[34] "The Lord needs it," they said. [35] Then they brought it to Jesus, and after throwing their clothes on the colt, they helped Jesus get on it. [36] As he was going along, they were spreading their clothes on the road. [37] Now he came near the path down the Mount of Olives, and the whole crowd of the disciples began to praise God joyfully with a loud voice for all the miracles they had seen:

NOTES

³⁸ Blessed is the King who comes
in the name of the Lord.
Peace in heaven
and glory in the highest heaven!

³⁹ Some of the Pharisees from the crowd told him, "Teacher, rebuke your disciples."

⁴⁰ He answered, "I tell you, if they were to keep silent, the stones would cry out."

JESUS'S LOVE FOR JERUSALEM

⁴¹ As he approached and saw the city, he wept for it, ⁴² saying, "If you knew this day what would bring peace—but now it is hidden from your eyes. ⁴³ For the days will come on you when your enemies will build a barricade around you, surround you, and hem you in on every side. ⁴⁴ They will crush you and your children among you to the ground, and they will not leave one stone on another in your midst, because you did not recognize the time when God visited you."

📖 GOING DEEPER

PSALM 118:25-29

²⁵ Lord, save us!
Lord, please grant us success!

²⁶ He who comes in the name of the Lord is blessed.

From the house of the Lord we bless you.
²⁷ The Lord is God and has given us light.
Bind the festival sacrifice with cords
to the horns of the altar.
²⁸ You are my God, and I will give you thanks.
You are my God; I will exalt you.
²⁹ Give thanks to the Lord, for he is good;
his faithful love endures forever.

ZECHARIAH 9:9

Rejoice greatly, Daughter Zion!
Shout in triumph, Daughter Jerusalem!
Look, your King is coming to you;
he is righteous and victorious,
humble and riding on a donkey,
on a colt, the foal of a donkey.

DAY 43

JESUS CLEANSES THE TEMPLE

SECTION 4

MARK 11:12-19

THE BARREN FIG TREE IS CURSED

[12] The next day when they went out from Bethany, he was hungry. [13] Seeing in the distance a fig tree with leaves, he went to find out if there was anything on it. When he came to it, he found nothing but leaves; for it was not the season for figs. [14] He said to it, "May no one ever eat fruit from you again!" And his disciples heard it.

CLEANSING THE TEMPLE

[15] They came to Jerusalem, and he went into the temple and began to throw out those buying and selling. He overturned the tables of the money changers and the chairs of those selling doves, [16] and would not permit anyone to carry goods through the temple.

[17] He was teaching them: "Is it not written, My house will be called a house of prayer for all nations? But you have made it a den of thieves!"

[18] The chief priests and the scribes heard it and started looking for a way to kill him. For they were afraid of him, because the whole crowd was astonished by his teaching.

[19] Whenever evening came, they would go out of the city.

GOING DEEPER

JEREMIAH 7:1-11

FALSE TRUST IN THE TEMPLE

[1] This is the word that came to Jeremiah from the Lord: [2] "Stand in the gate of the house of the Lord and there call out this word: 'Hear the word of the Lord, all you people of Judah who enter through these gates to worship the Lord.

[3] "'This is what the Lord of Armies, the God of Israel, says: Correct your ways and your actions, and I will allow you to live in this place. [4]

Do not trust deceitful words, chanting, "This is the temple of the Lord, the temple of the Lord, the temple of the Lord." ⁵ Instead, if you really correct your ways and your actions, if you act justly toward one another, ⁶ if you no longer oppress the resident alien, the fatherless, and the widow and no longer shed innocent blood in this place or follow other gods, bringing harm on yourselves, ⁷ I will allow you to live in this place, the land I gave to your ancestors long ago and forever. ⁸ But look, you keep trusting in deceitful words that cannot help.

⁹ "'Do you steal, murder, commit adultery, swear falsely, burn incense to Baal, and follow other gods that you have not known? ¹⁰ Then do you come and stand before me in this house that bears my name and say, "We are rescued, so we can continue doing all these detestable acts"? ¹¹ Has this house, which bears my name, become a den of robbers in your view? Yes, I too have seen it.

This is the Lord's declaration.'"

PSALM 69:7–9

⁷ For I have endured insults because of you,
and shame has covered my face.
⁸ I have become a stranger to my brothers
and a foreigner to my mother's sons
⁹ because zeal for your house has consumed me,
and the insults of those who insult you
have fallen on me.

NOTES

JESUS TEACHES IN THE TEMPLE

———

"HEAVEN AND EARTH WILL PASS AWAY, BUT MY WORDS WILL NEVER PASS AWAY."

LUKE 21:33

DAY 44   SECTION 4

LUKE 21

THE WIDOW'S GIFT

¹ He looked up and saw the rich dropping their offerings into the temple treasury. ² He also saw a poor widow dropping in two tiny coins. ³ "Truly I tell you," he said, "this poor widow has put in more than all of them. ⁴ For all these people have put in gifts out of their surplus, but she out of her poverty has put in all she had to live on."

DESTRUCTION OF THE TEMPLE PREDICTED

⁵ As some were talking about the temple, how it was adorned with beautiful stones and gifts dedicated to God, he said, ⁶ "These things that you see—the days will come when not one stone will be left on another that will not be thrown down."

SIGNS OF THE END OF THE AGE

⁷ "Teacher," they asked him, "so when will these things happen? And what will be the sign when these things are about to take place?"

⁸ Then he said, "Watch out that you are not deceived. For many will come in my name, saying, 'I am he,' and, 'The time is near.' Don't follow them. ⁹ When you hear of wars and rebellions, don't be alarmed. Indeed, it is necessary that these things take place first, but the end won't come right away."

¹⁰ Then he told them, "Nation will be raised up against nation, and kingdom against kingdom. ¹¹ There will be violent earthquakes, and famines and plagues in various places, and there will be terrifying sights and great signs from heaven. ¹² But before all these things, they will lay their hands on you and persecute you. They will hand you over to the synagogues and prisons, and you will be brought before kings and governors because of my name. ¹³ This will give you an opportunity to bear witness.

¹⁴ Therefore make up your minds not to prepare your defense ahead of time, ¹⁵ for I will give you such words and a wisdom that none of your adversaries will be able to resist or contradict.

NOTES

[16] You will even be betrayed by parents, brothers, relatives, and friends. They will kill some of you. [17] You will be hated by everyone because of my name, [18] but not a hair of your head will be lost. [19] By your endurance, gain your lives.

THE DESTRUCTION OF JERUSALEM

[20] "When you see Jerusalem surrounded by armies, then recognize that its desolation has come near. [21] Then those in Judea must flee to the mountains. Those inside the city must leave it, and those who are in the country must not enter it, [22] because these are days of vengeance to fulfill all the things that are written. [23] Woe to pregnant women and nursing mothers in those days, for there will be great distress in the land and wrath against this people. [24] They will be killed by the sword and be led captive into all the nations, and Jerusalem will be trampled by the Gentiles until the times of the Gentiles are fulfilled.

THE COMING OF THE SON OF MAN

[25] "Then there will be signs in the sun, moon, and stars; and there will be anguish on the earth among nations bewildered by the roaring of the sea and the waves. [26] People will faint from fear and expectation of the things that are coming on the world, because the powers of the heavens will be shaken. [27] Then they will see the Son of Man coming in a cloud with power and great glory. [28] But when these things begin to take place, stand up and lift your heads, because your redemption is near."

THE PARABLE OF THE FIG TREE

[29] Then he told them a parable: "Look at the fig tree, and all the trees. [30] As soon as they put out leaves you can see for yourselves and recognize that summer is already near. [31] In the same way, when you see these things happening, recognize that the kingdom of God is near. [32] Truly I tell you, this generation will certainly not pass away until all things take place. [33] Heaven and earth will pass away, but my words will never pass away.

THE NEED FOR WATCHFULNESS

[34] "Be on your guard, so that your minds are not dulled from carousing, drunkenness, and worries of life, or that day will come on you unexpectedly [35] like a trap. For it will come on all who live on the face

of the whole earth. ³⁶ But be alert at all times, praying that you may have strength to escape all these things that are going to take place and to stand before the Son of Man."

³⁷ During the day, he was teaching in the temple, but in the evening he would go out and spend the night on what is called the Mount of Olives. ³⁸ Then all the people would come early in the morning to hear him in the temple.

LUKE 22:1–2

THE PLOT TO KILL JESUS

¹ The Festival of Unleavened Bread, which is called Passover, was approaching. ² The chief priests and the scribes were looking for a way to put him to death, because they were afraid of the people.

GOING DEEPER

DANIEL 7:13–14

¹³ I continued watching in the night visions,

> and suddenly one like a son of man
> was coming with the clouds of heaven.
> He approached the Ancient of Days
> and was escorted before him.
> ¹⁴ He was given dominion
> and glory and a kingdom,
> so that those of every people,
> nation, and language
> should serve him.
> His dominion is an everlasting dominion
> that will not pass away,
> and his kingdom is one
> that will not be destroyed.

JESUS IS ANOINTED FOR BURIAL

DAY 45   SECTION 4

MATTHEW 26:14-16

¹⁴ Then one of the Twelve, the man called Judas Iscariot, went to the chief priests ¹⁵ and said, "What are you willing to give me if I hand him over to you?" So they weighed out thirty pieces of silver for him. ¹⁶ And from that time he started looking for a good opportunity to betray him.

MARK 14:3-11

THE ANOINTING AT BETHANY

³ While he was in Bethany at the house of Simon the leper, as he was reclining at the table, a woman came with an alabaster jar of very expensive perfume of pure nard. She broke the jar and poured it on his head. ⁴ But some were expressing indignation to one another: "Why has this perfume been wasted? ⁵ For this perfume might have been sold for more than three hundred denarii and given to the poor." And they began to scold her.

⁶ Jesus replied, "Leave her alone. Why are you bothering her?

She has done a noble thing for me.

⁷ You always have the poor with you, and you can do what is good for them whenever you want, but you do not always have me. ⁸ She has done what she could; she has anointed my body in advance for burial. ⁹ Truly I tell you, wherever the gospel is proclaimed in the whole world, what she has done will also be told in memory of her."

¹⁰ Then Judas Iscariot, one of the Twelve, went to the chief priests to betray Jesus to them. ¹¹ And when they heard this, they were glad and promised to give him money. So he started looking for a good opportunity to betray him.

LUKE 22:3-6

³ Then Satan entered Judas, called Iscariot, who was numbered among the Twelve. ⁴ He went away and discussed with the chief priests and temple police how he could hand him over to them. ⁵ They were glad and agreed to give him silver. ⁶ So he accepted the offer and started looking for a good opportunity to betray him to them when the crowd was not present.

◉ GOING DEEPER

PSALM 50:23

"Whoever offers a thanksgiving sacrifice honors me,
and whoever orders his conduct,
I will show him the salvation of God."

THE LAST SUPPER

DAY 46 — SECTION 4

MARK 14:12–72

PREPARATION FOR PASSOVER

¹² On the first day of Unleavened Bread, when they sacrifice the Passover lamb, his disciples asked him, "Where do you want us to go and prepare the Passover so that you may eat it?"

¹³ So he sent two of his disciples and told them, "Go into the city, and a man carrying a jar of water will meet you. Follow him. ¹⁴ Wherever he enters, tell the owner of the house, 'The Teacher says, "Where is my guest room where I may eat the Passover with my disciples?"' ¹⁵ He will show you a large room upstairs, furnished and ready. Make the preparations for us there." ¹⁶ So the disciples went out, entered the city, and found it just as he had told them, and they prepared the Passover.

BETRAYAL AT THE PASSOVER

¹⁷ When evening came, he arrived with the Twelve. ¹⁸ While they were reclining and eating, Jesus said, "Truly I tell you, one of you will betray me—one who is eating with me."

¹⁹ They began to be distressed and to say to him one by one, "Surely not I?"

²⁰ He said to them, "It is one of the Twelve—the one who is dipping bread in the bowl with me. ²¹ For the Son of Man will go just as it is written about him, but woe to that man by whom the Son of Man is betrayed! It would have been better for him if he had not been born."

NOTES

THE FIRST LORD'S SUPPER

²² As they were eating, he took bread, blessed and broke it, gave it to them, and said, "Take it; this is my body." ²³ Then he took a cup, and after giving thanks, he gave it to them, and they all drank from it. ²⁴ He said to them, "This is my blood of the covenant, which is poured out for many.

> ²⁵ Truly I tell you, I will no longer drink of the fruit of the vine until that day when I drink it new in the kingdom of God."

²⁶ After singing a hymn, they went out to the Mount of Olives.

PETER'S DENIAL PREDICTED

²⁷ Then Jesus said to them, "All of you will fall away, because it is written:

> I will strike the shepherd,
> and the sheep will be scattered.

²⁸ But after I have risen, I will go ahead of you to Galilee."

²⁹ Peter told him, "Even if everyone falls away, I will not."

³⁰ "Truly I tell you," Jesus said to him, "today, this very night, before the rooster crows twice, you will deny me three times."

³¹ But he kept insisting, "If I have to die with you, I will never deny you." And they all said the same thing.

THE PRAYER IN THE GARDEN

³² Then they came to a place named Gethsemane, and he told his disciples, "Sit here while I pray." ³³ He took Peter, James, and John with him, and he began to be deeply distressed and troubled. ³⁴ He said to them, "I am deeply grieved to the point of death. Remain here and stay awake." ³⁵ He went a little farther, fell to the ground, and prayed that if it were possible, the hour might pass from him. ³⁶ And he said, *"Abba,* Father! All things are possible for you. Take this cup away from me. Nevertheless, not what I will, but what you will." ³⁷ Then he came and found them sleeping. He said to Peter, "Simon, are you sleeping? Couldn't you stay awake one hour? ³⁸ Stay awake and pray so that you won't enter into temptation.

The spirit is willing, but the flesh is weak." ³⁹ Once again he went away and prayed, saying the same thing. ⁴⁰ And again he came and found them sleeping, because they could not keep their eyes open. They did not know what to say to him. ⁴¹ Then he came a third time and said to them, "Are you still sleeping and resting? Enough! The time has come. See, the Son of Man is betrayed into the hands of sinners. ⁴² Get up; let's go. See, my betrayer is near."

JUDAS'S BETRAYAL OF JESUS

⁴³ While he was still speaking, Judas, one of the Twelve, suddenly arrived. With him was a mob, with swords and clubs, from the chief priests, the scribes, and the elders. ⁴⁴ His betrayer had given them a signal. "The one I kiss," he said, "he's the one; arrest him and take him away under guard." ⁴⁵ So when he came, immediately he went up to Jesus and said, "Rabbi!" and kissed him. ⁴⁶ They took hold of him and arrested him. ⁴⁷ One of those who stood by drew his sword, struck the high priest's servant, and cut off his ear.

⁴⁸ Jesus said to them, "Have you come out with swords and clubs, as if I were a criminal, to capture me? ⁴⁹ Every day I was among you, teaching in the temple, and you didn't arrest me. But the Scriptures must be fulfilled."

⁵⁰ Then they all deserted him and ran away. ⁵¹ Now a certain young man, wearing nothing but a linen cloth, was following him. They caught hold of him, ⁵² but he left the linen cloth behind and ran away naked.

JESUS FACES THE SANHEDRIN

⁵³ They led Jesus away to the high priest, and all the chief priests, the elders, and the scribes assembled. ⁵⁴ Peter followed him at a distance, right into the high priest's courtyard. He was sitting with the servants, warming himself by the fire.

⁵⁵ The chief priests and the whole Sanhedrin were looking for testimony against Jesus to put him to death, but they could not find any. ⁵⁶ For many were giving false testimony against him, and the testimonies did not agree. ⁵⁷ Some stood up and gave false testimony against him, stating, ⁵⁸ "We heard him say, 'I will destroy this temple made with human hands, and in three days I will build another not made by hands.'" ⁵⁹ Yet their testimony did not agree even on this.

NOTES

⁶⁰ Then the high priest stood up before them all and questioned Jesus, "Don't you have an answer to what these men are testifying against you?" ⁶¹ But he kept silent and did not answer. Again the high priest questioned him, "Are you the Messiah, the Son of the Blessed One?"

⁶² "I am," said Jesus, "and you will see the Son of Man seated at the right hand of Power and coming with the clouds of heaven."

⁶³ Then the high priest tore his robes and said, "Why do we still need witnesses? ⁶⁴ You have heard the blasphemy. What is your decision?" They all condemned him as deserving death.

⁶⁵ Then some began to spit on him, to blindfold him, and to beat him, saying, "Prophesy!" The temple servants also took him and slapped him.

PETER DENIES HIS LORD

⁶⁶ While Peter was in the courtyard below, one of the high priest's maidservants came. ⁶⁷ When she saw Peter warming himself, she looked at him and said, "You also were with Jesus, the man from Nazareth."

⁶⁸ But he denied it: "I don't know or understand what you're talking about." Then he went out to the entryway, and a rooster crowed.

⁶⁹ When the maidservant saw him again, she began to tell those standing nearby, "This man is one of them."

⁷⁰ But again he denied it. After a little while those standing there said to Peter again, "You certainly are one of them, since you're also a Galilean."

⁷¹ Then he started to curse and swear, "I don't know this man you're talking about!"

⁷² Immediately a rooster crowed a second time, and Peter remembered when Jesus had spoken the word to him, "Before the rooster crows twice, you will deny me three times." And he broke down and wept.

JOHN 16:16–24, 32-33

SORROW TURNED TO JOY

¹⁶ "In a little while, you will no longer see me; again in a little while, you will see me."

¹⁷ Then some of his disciples said to one another, "What is this he's telling us: 'In a little while, you will not see me; again in a little while, you will see me,' and, 'Because I am going to the Father'?" ¹⁸ They said, "What is this he is saying, 'In a little while'? We don't know what he's talking about."

¹⁹ Jesus knew they wanted to ask him, and so he said to them, "Are you asking one another about what I said, 'In a little while, you will not see me; again in a little while, you will see me'? ²⁰ Truly I tell you, you will weep and mourn, but the world will rejoice. You will become sorrowful, but your sorrow will turn to joy. ²¹ When a woman is in labor, she has pain because her time has come. But when she has given birth to a child, she no longer remembers the suffering because of the joy that a person has been born into the world. ²² So you also have sorrow now. But I will see you again. Your hearts will rejoice, and no one will take away your joy from you.

²³ "In that day you will not ask me anything. Truly I tell you, anything you ask the Father in my name, he will give you. ²⁴ Until now you have asked for nothing in my name. Ask and you will receive, so that your joy may be complete."

…

³² "Indeed, an hour is coming, and has come, when each of you will be scattered to his own home, and you will leave me alone. Yet I am not alone, because the Father is with me. ³³ I have told you these things so that in me you may have peace. You will have suffering in this world. Be courageous! I have conquered the world."

GOING DEEPER

PSALM 41:7-13

⁷ All who hate me whisper together about me;
they plan to harm me.
⁸ "Something awful has overwhelmed him,
and he won't rise again from where he lies!"
⁹ Even my friend in whom I trusted,
one who ate my bread,
has raised his heel against me.

¹⁰ But you, Lord, be gracious to me and raise me up;
then I will repay them.
¹¹ By this I know that you delight in me:
my enemy does not shout in triumph over me.
¹² You supported me because of my integrity
and set me in your presence forever.

¹³ Blessed be the Lord God of Israel,
from everlasting to everlasting.
Amen and amen.

NOTES

GOOD FRIDAY

AND JESUS CALLED OUT
WITH A LOUD VOICE,
"FATHER, INTO YOUR HANDS I
ENTRUST MY SPIRIT." SAYING
THIS, HE BREATHED HIS LAST.

LUKE 23:46

DAY 47   SECTION 4

LUKE 23:1-53

JESUS FACES PILATE

¹ Then their whole assembly rose up and brought him before Pilate. ² They began to accuse him, saying, "We found this man misleading our nation, opposing payment of taxes to Caesar, and saying that he himself is the Messiah, a king."

³ So Pilate asked him, "Are you the king of the Jews?"

He answered him, "You say so."

⁴ Pilate then told the chief priests and the crowds, "I find no grounds for charging this man."

⁵ But they kept insisting, "He stirs up the people, teaching throughout all Judea, from Galilee where he started even to here."

JESUS FACES HEROD ANTIPAS

⁶ When Pilate heard this, he asked if the man was a Galilean. ⁷ Finding that he was under Herod's jurisdiction, he sent him to Herod, who was also in Jerusalem during those days. ⁸ Herod was very glad to see Jesus; for a long time he had wanted to see him because he had heard about him and was hoping to see some miracle performed by him. ⁹ So he kept asking him questions, but Jesus did not answer him. ¹⁰ The chief priests and the scribes stood by, vehemently accusing him. ¹¹ Then Herod, with his soldiers, treated him with contempt, mocked him, dressed him in bright clothing, and sent him back to Pilate. ¹² That very day Herod and Pilate became friends. Previously, they had been enemies.

JESUS OR BARABBAS

¹³ Pilate called together the chief priests, the leaders, and the people, ¹⁴ and said to them, "You have brought me this man as one who misleads the people. But in fact, after examining him in your presence, I have found no grounds to charge this man with those things you accuse him of. ¹⁵ Neither has Herod, because he sent him back to us. Clearly, he has done nothing to deserve death. ¹⁶ Therefore, I will have him whipped and then release him."

¹⁸ Then they all cried out together, "Take this man away! Release Barabbas to us!" ¹⁹ (He had been thrown into prison for a rebellion that had taken place in the city, and for murder.)

NOTES

²⁰ Wanting to release Jesus, Pilate addressed them again, ²¹ but they kept shouting, "Crucify! Crucify him!"

²² A third time he said to them, "Why? What has this man done wrong? I have found in him no grounds for the death penalty. Therefore, I will have him whipped and then release him."

²³ But they kept up the pressure, demanding with loud voices that he be crucified, and their voices won out. ²⁴ So Pilate decided to grant their demand ²⁵ and released the one they were asking for, who had been thrown into prison for rebellion and murder. But he handed Jesus over to their will.

THE WAY TO THE CROSS

²⁶ As they led him away, they seized Simon, a Cyrenian, who was coming in from the country, and laid the cross on him to carry behind Jesus. ²⁷ A large crowd of people followed him, including women who were mourning and lamenting him. ²⁸ But turning to them, Jesus said, "Daughters of Jerusalem, do not weep for me, but weep for yourselves and your children. ²⁹ Look, the days are coming when they will say, 'Blessed are the women without children, the wombs that never bore, and the breasts that never nursed!' ³⁰ Then they will begin to say to the mountains, 'Fall on us!' and to the hills, 'Cover us!' ³¹ For if they do these things when the wood is green, what will happen when it is dry?"

CRUCIFIED BETWEEN TWO CRIMINALS

³² Two others—criminals—were also led away to be executed with him. ³³ When they arrived at the place called The Skull, they crucified him there, along with the criminals, one on the right and one on the left. ³⁴ Then Jesus said, "Father, forgive them, because they do not know what they are doing." And they divided his clothes and cast lots.

³⁵ The people stood watching, and even the leaders were scoffing: "He saved others; let him save himself if this is God's Messiah, the Chosen One!" ³⁶ The soldiers also mocked him. They came offering him sour wine ³⁷ and said, "If you are the king of the Jews, save yourself!"

³⁸ An inscription was above him: THIS IS THE KING OF THE JEWS.

³⁹ Then one of the criminals hanging there began to yell insults at him: "Aren't you the Messiah? Save yourself and us!"

⁴⁰ But the other answered, rebuking him: "Don't you even fear God, since you are undergoing the same punishment? ⁴¹ We are punished justly, because we're getting back what we deserve for the things we did, but this man has done nothing wrong." ⁴² Then he said, "Jesus, remember me when you come into your kingdom."

⁴³ And he said to him, "Truly I tell you, today you will be with me in paradise."

THE DEATH OF JESUS

⁴⁴ It was now about noon, and darkness came over the whole land until three, ⁴⁵ because the sun's light failed. The curtain of the sanctuary was split down the middle. ⁴⁶ And Jesus called out with a loud voice, "Father, into your hands I entrust my spirit." Saying this, he breathed his last.

> ⁴⁷ When the centurion saw what happened, he began to glorify God, saying, "This man really was righteous!"

⁴⁸ All the crowds that had gathered for this spectacle, when they saw what had taken place, went home, striking their chests. ⁴⁹ But all who knew him, including the women who had followed him from Galilee, stood at a distance, watching these things.

THE BURIAL OF JESUS

⁵⁰ There was a good and righteous man named Joseph, a member of the Sanhedrin, ⁵¹ who had not agreed with their plan and action. He was from Arimathea, a Judean town, and was looking forward to the kingdom of God. ⁵² He approached Pilate and asked for Jesus's body. ⁵³ Taking it down, he wrapped it in fine linen and placed it in a tomb cut into the rock, where no one had ever been placed.

GOING DEEPER

HEBREWS 10:10

By this will, we have been sanctified through the offering of the body of Jesus Christ once for all time.

HYMN

WHEN I SURVEY THE WONDROUS CROSS

WORDS: ISAAC WATTS
MUSIC: LOWELL MASON

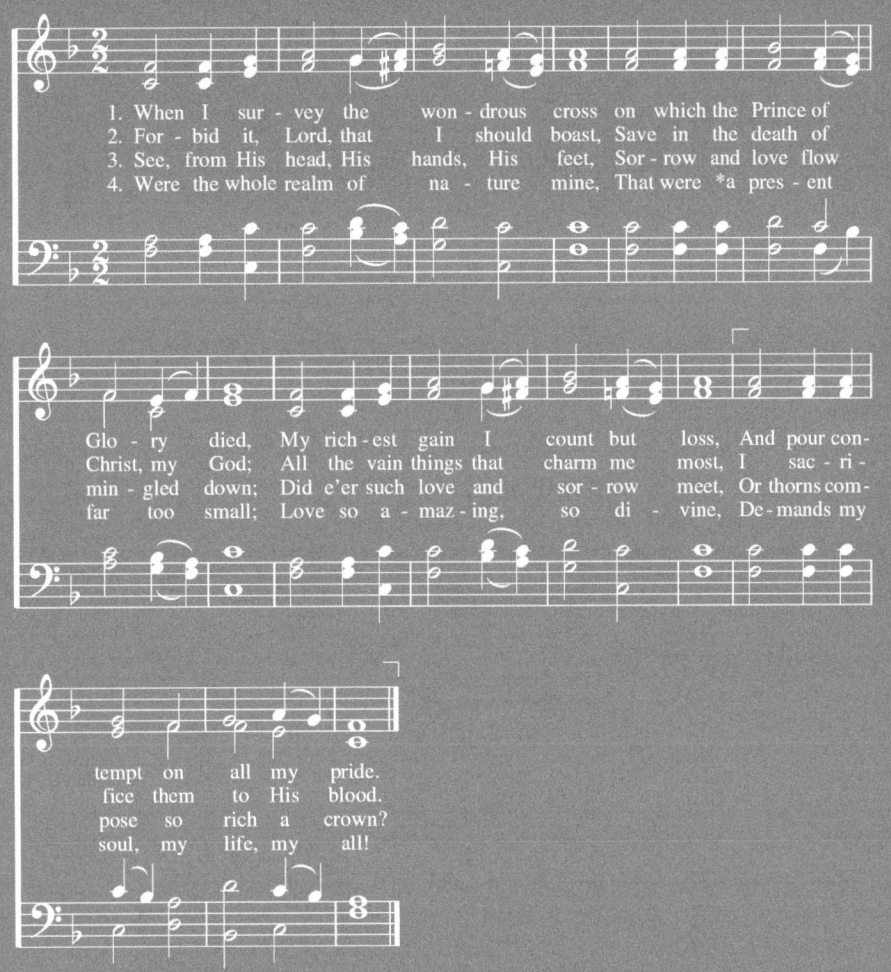

DAY 48

HOLY SATURDAY

SECTION 4

MATTHEW 27:62-66

THE CLOSELY GUARDED TOMB

⁶² The next day, which followed the preparation day, the chief priests and the Pharisees gathered before Pilate ⁶³ and said, "Sir, we remember that while this deceiver was still alive he said, 'After three days I will rise again.' ⁶⁴ So give orders that the tomb be made secure until the third day. Otherwise, his disciples may come, steal him, and tell the people, 'He has been raised from the dead,' and the last deception will be worse than the first."

⁶⁵ "Take guards," Pilate told them.

> "Go and make it as secure as you know how."

⁶⁶ They went and secured the tomb by setting a seal on the stone and placing the guards.

LUKE 23:54-56

⁵⁴ It was the preparation day, and the Sabbath was about to begin. ⁵⁵ The women who had come with him from Galilee followed along and observed the tomb and how his body was placed. ⁵⁶ Then they returned and prepared spices and perfumes. And they rested on the Sabbath according to the commandment.

◼ GOING DEEPER

PSALM 130:5-8

⁵ I wait for the Lord; I wait
and put my hope in his word.
⁶ I wait for the Lord
more than watchmen for the morning—
more than watchmen for the morning.

⁷ Israel, put your hope in the Lord.
For there is faithful love with the Lord,
and with him is redemption in abundance.
⁸ And he will redeem Israel
from all its iniquities.

I have seen the Lord!

John 20:18

DAY 49   SECTION 4

EASTER SUNDAY

JOHN 20

THE EMPTY TOMB

¹ On the first day of the week Mary Magdalene came to the tomb early, while it was still dark. She saw that the stone had been removed from the tomb. ² So she went running to Simon Peter and to the other disciple, the one Jesus loved, and said to them, "They've taken the Lord out of the tomb, and we don't know where they've put him!"

³ At that, Peter and the other disciple went out, heading for the tomb. ⁴ The two were running together, but the other disciple outran Peter and got to the tomb first. ⁵ Stooping down, he saw the linen cloths lying there, but he did not go in. ⁶ Then, following him, Simon Peter also came. He entered the tomb and saw the linen cloths lying there. ⁷ The wrapping that had been on his head was not lying with the linen cloths but was folded up in a separate place by itself. ⁸ The other disciple, who had reached the tomb first, then also went in, saw, and believed. ⁹ For they did not yet understand the Scripture that he must rise from the dead. ¹⁰ Then the disciples returned to the place where they were staying.

MARY MAGDALENE SEES THE RISEN LORD

¹¹ But Mary stood outside the tomb, crying. As she was crying, she stooped to look into the tomb. ¹² She saw two angels in white sitting where Jesus's body had been lying, one at the head and the other at the feet. ¹³ They said to her, "Woman, why are you crying?"

"Because they've taken away my Lord," she told them, "and I don't know where they've put him."

¹⁴ Having said this, she turned around and saw Jesus standing there, but she did not know it was Jesus. ¹⁵ "Woman," Jesus said to her, "why are you crying? Who is it that you're seeking?"

Supposing he was the gardener, she replied, "Sir, if you've carried him away, tell me where you've put him, and I will take him away."

¹⁶ Jesus said to her, "Mary."

Turning around, she said to him in Aramaic, *"Rabboni!"*—which means "Teacher."

¹⁷ "Don't cling to me," Jesus told her, "since I have not yet ascended to the Father. But go to my brothers and tell them that I am ascending to my Father and your Father, to my God and your God."

¹⁸ Mary Magdalene went and announced to the disciples, "I have seen the Lord!" And she told them what he had said to her.

THE DISCIPLES COMMISSIONED

¹⁹ When it was evening on that first day of the week, the disciples were gathered together with the doors locked because they feared the Jews. Jesus came, stood among them, and said to them, "Peace be with you."

²⁰ Having said this, he showed them his hands and his side. So the disciples rejoiced when they saw the Lord.

²¹ Jesus said to them again, "Peace be with you. As the Father has sent me, I also send you." ²² After saying this, he breathed on them and said, "Receive the Holy Spirit. ²³ If you forgive the sins of any, they are forgiven them; if you retain the sins of any, they are retained."

THOMAS SEES AND BELIEVES

²⁴ But Thomas (called "Twin"), one of the Twelve, was not with them when Jesus came. ²⁵ So the other disciples were telling him, "We've seen the Lord!"

But he said to them, "If I don't see the mark of the nails in his hands, put my finger into the mark of the nails, and put my hand into his side, I will never believe."

²⁶ A week later his disciples were indoors again, and Thomas was with them. Even though the doors were locked, Jesus came and stood among them and said, "Peace be with you."

²⁷ Then he said to Thomas, "Put your finger here and look at my hands. Reach out your hand and put it into my side. Don't be faithless, but believe."

²⁸ Thomas responded to him, "My Lord and my God!"

²⁹ Jesus said, "Because you have seen me, you have believed. Blessed are those who have not seen and yet believe."

THE PURPOSE OF THIS GOSPEL

³⁰ Jesus performed many other signs in the presence of his disciples that are not written in this book. ³¹ But these are written so that you may believe that Jesus is the Messiah, the Son of God, and that by believing you may have life in his name.

◆ GOING DEEPER

PSALM 16:9-11

⁹ Therefore my heart is glad
and my whole being rejoices;
my body also rests securely.
¹⁰ For you will not abandon me to Sheol;
you will not allow your faithful one to see decay.
¹¹ You reveal the path of life to me;
in your presence is abundant joy;
at your right hand are eternal pleasures.

NOTES

BENEDICTION

I WILL MAKE KNOWN THE LORD'S FAITHFUL LOVE AND THE LORD'S PRAISEWORTHY ACTS, BECAUSE OF ALL THE LORD HAS DONE FOR US—EVEN THE MANY GOOD THINGS HE HAS DONE FOR THE HOUSE OF ISRAEL, WHICH HE DID FOR THEM BASED ON HIS COMPASSION AND THE ABUNDANCE OF HIS FAITHFUL LOVE.

ISAIAH 63:7

Tips for Memorizing Scripture

At He Reads Truth, we believe Scripture memorization is an important discipline in your walk with God. Committing God's Truth to memory means we carry it with us and we can minister to others wherever we go. As you approach the Weekly Truth verse in this book, try these memorization tips to see which techniques work best for you.

STUDY IT

Study the passage in its biblical context, and ask yourself a few questions before you begin to memorize it: What does this passage say? What does it mean? How would I say this in my own words? What does it teach me about God? Understanding what the passage means helps you know why it is important to carry it with you wherever you go.

Break the passage into smaller sections, memorizing a phrase at a time.

PRAY IT

Use the passage you are memorizing as a prompt for prayer.

WRITE IT

Dedicate a notebook to Scripture memorization, and write the passage over and over again.

Diagram the passage after you write it out. Place a square around the verbs, underline the nouns, and circle any adjectives or adverbs. Say the passage aloud several times, emphasizing the verbs as you repeat it. Then do the same thing again with the nouns, then the adjectives and adverbs.

Write out the first letter of each word in the passage somewhere you can reference it throughout the week as you work on your memorization.

Use a whiteboard to write out the passage. Erase a few words at a time as you continue to repeat it aloud. Keep erasing parts of the passage until you have it all committed to memory.

CREATE

If you can, make up a tune for the passage to sing as you go about your day, or try singing it to the tune of a favorite song.

Use hand signals or signs to come up with associations for each word or phrase and repeat the movements as you practice.

SAY IT

Repeat the passage out loud to yourself as you are going through the rhythm of your day—getting ready, pouring your coffee, waiting in traffic, or making dinner.

Listen to the passage read aloud to you.

Record a voice memo on your phone, and listen to it throughout the day or play it on an audio Bible.

SHARE IT

Memorize the passage with a friend, family member, or mentor. Spontaneously challenge each other to recite the passage, or pick a time to review your passage and practice saying it from memory together.

Send the passage as an encouraging text to a friend, testing yourself as you type to see how much you have memorized so far.

KEEP AT IT

Set reminders on your phone to prompt you to practice your passage.

Keep a stack of note cards with Scripture you are memorizing by your bed. Practice reciting what you've memorized previously before you go to sleep, ending with the passages you are currently learning. If you wake up in the middle of the night, review them again instead of grabbing your phone. Read them out loud before you get out of bed in the morning.

CSB BOOK ABBREVIATIONS

OLD TESTAMENT

GN Genesis	**JB** Job	**HAB** Habakkuk	**PHP** Philippians
EX Exodus	**PS** Psalms	**ZPH** Zephaniah	**COL** Colossians
LV Leviticus	**PR** Proverbs	**HG** Haggai	**1TH** 1 Thessalonians
NM Numbers	**EC** Ecclesiastes	**ZCH** Zechariah	**2TH** 2 Thessalonians
DT Deuteronomy	**SG** Song of Solomon	**MAL** Malachi	**1TM** 1 Timothy
JOS Joshua	**IS** Isaiah		**2TM** 2 Timothy
JDG Judges	**JR** Jeremiah	**NEW TESTAMENT**	**TI** Titus
RU Ruth	**LM** Lamentations	**MT** Matthew	**PHM** Philemon
1SM 1 Samuel	**EZK** Ezekiel	**MK** Mark	**HEB** Hebrews
2SM 2 Samuel	**DN** Daniel	**LK** Luke	**JMS** James
1KG 1 Kings	**HS** Hosea	**JN** John	**1PT** 1 Peter
2KG 2 Kings	**JL** Joel	**AC** Acts	**2PT** 2 Peter
1CH 1 Chronicles	**AM** Amos	**RM** Romans	**1JN** 1 John
2CH 2 Chronicles	**OB** Obadiah	**1CO** 1 Corinthians	**2JN** 2 John
EZR Ezra	**JNH** Jonah	**2CO** 2 Corinthians	**3JN** 3 John
NEH Nehemiah	**MC** Micah	**GL** Galatians	**JD** Jude
EST Esther	**NAH** Nahum	**EPH** Ephesians	**RV** Revelation

BIBLIOGRAPHY

Barry, John D. "Isaiah, Book of." In *The Lexham Bible Dictionary*, edited by John D. Barry et al. Bellingham: Lexham Press, 2016.

Duvall, J. Scott, and J. Daniel Hays. *Grasping God's Word*. Grand Rapids: Zondervan, 2020.

House, Paul R. *Old Testament Theology*. Downers Grove: InterVarsity Press, 1998.

Mosley, Harold, and Steve Bond. "Isaiah, Book of." In *Holman Illustrated Bible Dictionary*, edited by Chad Brand et al. Nashville: Holman Bible Publishers, 2003.

Names of God. Bellingham: Faithlife, 2015.

YOUR DAILY GUIDE TO READING GOD'S WORD

AUTOMATICALLY DELIVERED TO YOU EACH AND EVERY MONTH

If you are looking to establish a habit of daily Bible reading or to grow in your knowledge and understanding of Scripture, look no further. Sign up today and receive our latest Daily Reading Guide delivered to your doorstep monthly.

HE READS TRUTH

LEARN MORE AND SUBSCRIBE AT
SHOPSHEREADSTRUTH.COM/HRTLENT24

FOR THE RECORD: HE WILL SAVE US

You just spent 49 days in the Word of God.

My favorite day of this reading plan:

One thing I learned about God:

What was God doing in my life during this study?

How did I find delight in God's Word?

What did I learn that I want to share with someone else?

A specific passage or verse that encouraged me:

A specific passage or verse that challenged and convicted me: